W9-BPN-001

XP6P

Nomadic Empires

FROM MONGOLIA TO THE DANUBE

NOMADIC EMPIRES

GERARD CHALIAND

TRANSLATED FROM THE FRENCH BY
A.M. BERRETT

TRANSACTION PUBLISHERS
NEW BRUNSWICK (U.S.A.) AND LONDON (U.K.)

DS
329.4
C4813
2004

c, l

LIBRARY OF CONGRESS
NOV 2 6 2003 N
COPY____
COPYRIGHT OFFICE

#52348837

9-28-05

Copyright © 2004 by Transaction Publishers, New Brunswick, New Jersey.

All rights reserved under International and Pan-American Copyright Conventions. No part of this book may be reproduced or transmitted in any form or by any means, electronic or mechanical, including photocopy, recording, or any information storage and retrieval system, without prior permission in writing from the publisher. All inquiries should be addressed to Transaction Publishers, Rutgers—The State University, 35 Berrue Circle, Piscataway, New Jersey 08854-8042.

This book is printed on acid-free paper that meets the American National Standard for Permanence of Paper for Printed Library Materials.

Library of Congress Catalog Number: 2003053340
ISBN: 0-7658-0204-X
Printed in the United States of America

Library of Congress Cataloging-in-Publication Data

Chaliand, Gérard, 1934-
    [Empires nomades de la Mongolie au Danube. English]
    Nomadic empires : from Mongolia to the Danube / Gerard Chaliand; translated from the French by A.M. Berrett.
        p. cm.
    Includes bibliographical references and index.
    ISBN 0-7658-0204-X (cloth : alk. paper)
        1. Asia, Central—History. 2. Nomads—Asia, Central—History. 3. Eurasia—History. I. Title.

DS329.4.C4813 2003
958'.01—dc21

                                                                2003053340

To the memory of my friend Amilcar Cabral (1924-1973)
with whom I did my apprenticeship in Guinea-Bissau

I say to you with confidence, if your peasants, I will not say Kings and knights, were willing to go as do the Kings of the Tartars and to be content with the same kind of food, they could take possession of the whole world.

—William of RUBRUCK
(Franciscan emissary from the French king Louis IX
to the Mongols, 13th century)
"The Journey of William of Rubruck,"
in *The Mongol Mission*

Sedentary people have become used to laziness and ease. They are sunk in well-being and luxury. They have entrusted the defence of their property and their lives to the governor and ruler who rules them, and to the militia which has the task of guarding them...

The Bedouins, on the other hand, live apart from the community. They are alone in the country and remote from militias. They have no walls or gates. Therefore, they provide their own defence and do not entrust it to, or rely upon others for it. They always carry weapons. They watch carefully all sides of the road. They take hurried naps only when they are together in company or when they are in the saddle. They pay attention to the most distant barking...

Fortitude has become a character quality of theirs, and courage their nature.

—Ibn Khaldun, *The Muqaddimah*

...there are two ways in which wars come about. Sometimes they are due to the ambition of princes or of republics which are seeking to set up an empire; under which head fall the wars waged by Alexander the Great and those waged by the Romans, and those which are continually being waged by this power and that. Such wars are dangerous, but they do not entirely remove the inhabitants of the country invaded; for the victor is content provided its people become subject to his obedience, often lets them keep their own laws, and always leaves them their houses and their chattels. The other way in which war is brought about is when a whole people with all its families leaves a place, driven thence either by

famine or by war, and sets out to look for a new home and a new country in which to live. In this case it does not, as in the previous case, merely govern there, but it takes possession of every single thing, and expels or kills the old inhabitants. This is war of the most cruel and terrifying kind...

Peoples such as these quit their own lands when constrained to do so by necessity, as had been said above; and the necessity is due either to famine or to a war or to hardships undergone in their own country; for in such a case they are constrained to go in search of new lands. And such peoples when they are very numerous and then make an incursion into the lands of others, kill the inhabitants, seize their goods, and establish a new kingdom under a new name...

Peoples, therefore, who have been driven out by sheer necessity, are very formidable, and unless confronted by good armies, can never be held back...

The larger migrations, involving whole peoples, have come from Scythia, a country that is cold and poor. In it, when the population becomes large, the land is not fertile enough to sustain it, and they are forced to emigrate; for there are many causes to drive them out and none to keep them at home..."

—Machiavelli, *The Discourses*, VIII, 2

Contents

Foreword

Few areas have been and remain as marked by Western-centeredness as the area of military writing. It is simply amazing that there has been no work in French, English, or, to my knowledge, German devoted to the military history of the Ottoman Empire in the last fifty years. Yet, from the fourteenth to the seventeenth century, that empire was an extremely redoubtable adversary for the states of Europe, and more particularly for the Hapsburg states.

The present work originated in the research I did in preparation for my book, *The Art of War in World History* (University of California Press. Foreword by General Lucien Poirier) in which I brought together the thinkers and strategic cultures of the Byzantines, China, India and the Muslims.

In doing so, as that "universal strategic library," as Lucien Poirier described it, came together, I began to feel that the military role of the Altaic nomads of central Asia had been seriously underestimated by military historians and, indeed, by historians in general. For two thousand years, from the fourth century B.C. to the fifteenth century A.D., the steppe areas of High Asia, from the borders of Manchuria to Ukraine, were the "zone of turbulence," threatening settled peoples from China to Russia and Hungary, including Iran, India, the Byzantine empire, and even Egypt. It was thus a real *world stage* that was affected by these destructive nomads, who were yet sometimes constructive when, in two or three generations, they had assimilated the knowledge and culture in the widest sense of settled societies. China, Iran and Byzantium played key roles in that process of acculturation. Western Europe hardly experienced the permanent obsession with the pressure and incursions of nomads and even less—apart from the Iberian peninsula—the long foreign occupation that was the lot of Russia or the Balkans. Apart from the Viking raids, five centuries elapsed between the incursion of Attila and those of the Hungarians at the beginning of the tenth century, after which western Europe did not experience any further external invasions.

But this little tip of land was a fortunate exception. Over the rest of the Eurasian land-mass, the opposition between nomads emerging from central Asia and settled societies was, for two millennia, the essential foundation of world geopolitics.

This volume is written using a geopolitical and strategic approach in order to elicit the fundamental military importance of the nomadic Altaic peoples. It is, in short, an introduction to the military history of the peoples of central Asia and, above all, to the impact they had on world history over the span of two millennia.

They were peoples without a common language, most of them without writing, of diverse ethnic origins although belonging to a number of major branches (Turks, Mongols, Manchus, and their ancestors)—not to mention religious beliefs—but united by a common strategic culture, which can already be found among the Scythians who preceded them. It was a culture of the steppe, based on the mobility of the mounted archer using harassment and indirect maneuver before delivering the blow. It was a strategic culture that developed the capacity to concentrate far from bases and overcome problems of logistics infinitely more easily than did settled peoples.

Empire-destroyers when they managed to unite under the leadership of a brilliant commander, and sometimes empire-builders when they had been civilized by settled peoples, the heirs to the nomads—apart from the ravages they committed—contributed during what is known as the "Mongol peace" to exchanges along the "silk road" between China and the West, to which Marco Polo and ibn Battuta, among others, bear witness. These heirs were, for example, the builders of Samarqand and they successfully laid the bases of the great empires of the Ottomans and of the Mughals in India, to mention only the most recent ones.

In the military perspective in which this volume is written, it can be said that between the Roman legions and Bonaparte, no army surpassed the strategic effectiveness of the sons of the steppe. Indeed, only rarely were they even equaled.

1

Introduction

The Impact of the Nomads

History, as it is understood today, has been largely written using the framework of the nation-state or the great classical empires. There has been very little interest in the geographical entity of central Eurasia,[1] which sprawls across the steppes from the confines of Manchuria to Ukraine and peters out in the grassy plains of Hungary.

Why should we concern ourselves with a host of peoples whose names hardly anyone has heard of, who built empires that were often only short-lived, and whose histories are generally known only to us through the testimony of their adversaries?

If little attention has been paid to these societies and this geographical area, it is because they were not embodied in a state or in an enduring empire with more or less fixed borders and even less in a people. The various empires that came into being in High Asia or that originated there are simply not written about as is the Roman empire. No single people can claim the considerable heritage—one that is possibly unique in the military sphere—of the nomads of High Asia.

Nomad empires refer to those imperial nomads who emerged from central Eurasia, conquering mounted archers, some of them famous, such as Attila, Genghis Khan, or Timur (Tamerlane), who, over a period of two thousand years, made their mark on the history of the world.

Perhaps it could be said that, over the long run, the history of High Asia is the history of those who are dubbed Barbarians. They occupied not only the steppe but also part of the taïga with its dense coniferous forests. This vast area is larger than the size of the United States. It is cut up by high mountains and deserts, and, in the area of modern Mongolia, historically its manpower reserve, its climate is exceedingly harsh. Nature and the living conditions that prevail there produced a type of man who was hardy and predatory.

1

The prime determinant of the whole history of central Eurasia was the need for nomadic shepherds to have grazing land for their animals—which in return supplied them with their requirements. But what makes the history of these Barbarians important and, militarily, fundamental, is the role of *troublemaker* that they played over a period of more than two thousand years in the Eurasian landmass, and, from Antiquity to the fourteenth-fifteenth centuries, that area, together with the area around the Mediterranean, was the world stage of conflicts. In fact, High Asia was, until the appearance of what we call modern times, the *geopolitical pivot* of the ancient and medieval world and its *zone of turbulence*. In the long-term perspective, the geopolitical opposition is not, as is thought in the modern West, between sea empires and continental empires—as was sketched out by the British geopolitician Halford Mackinder in 1904—but between *nomads* and *settled peoples*. On the whole, the societies of High Asia based on nomadism and raiding were predatory. For them to become dangerous to their settled neighbors required that a leader emerge among them capable of uniting the various tribes of a group for some considerable period. That is what was achieved by the greatest among them, Genghis Khan, the creator of the largest empire in history.

Of course, history has seen nomads other than those of High Asia whose role was decisive or important. First and foremost there were the Bedouin of Arabia who, borne by a universalist monotheism, permanently transformed the world (but one may legitimately wonder whether it is possible to regard this warrior Islam, which very rapidly created urban civilizations, as a nomad society). Then there were the nomads of the sea such as the Vikings and the Varangians, the latter the creators of Kievan Rus. But, in terms of duration, no area had the military importance of High Asia whose nomadic waves caused the ancient and medieval world to tremble, from China to the West, including Iran, India, Byzantium, Russia and the Balkans. From the Scythians in the sixth century B.C. to the Manchus who made themselves masters of China in the middle of the seventeenth century, the military role of the nomads of central Eurasia was of capital importance. The mounted archer of High Asia took the art of warfare, especially at the time of Genghis Khan, to a degree of perfection that, in terms of logistics, maneuver, mobility, capacity to concentrate, shock, and firepower (bow-power serving as such), was equaled in the West only with Napoleon. And even in the matter of mobility, it was not until the Second World War and the tank-based *Blitzkrieg* that better was seen.

In the period of over two and a half thousand years that we are dealing with here, the nomadic populations of Eurasia amount broadly to a few main groupings: the Indo-Iranians, such as the Scythians who were eliminated from central Asia in the first centuries A.D., and the ancestors especially of the Turkic-speaking peoples, the Mongols and the Manchus; and, second, the so-called Uralo-Altaic peoples such as the Finns or the Hungarians.

Eastern High Asia—Mongolia in the broad sense—is the geographical origin of most of these peoples, and particularly of the Turkic-Mongols. While, throughout history, China had fascinated the nomads in the north and often suffered their attacks, the general movement of nomads took them westward. Population pressure found an outlet there and, in that respect, the Turkic-speakers played a key role.

As early as the second and third centuries A.D., Turkic-speaking peoples were moving westward, driving out or absorbing the Indo-Iranians and occupying the area known as Turkestan. From Transoxiana nomadic Turkish tribes gradually penetrated the settled periphery: Khurasan, western Iran, Asia Minor, and the Volga basin—this last starting in the ninth-eleventh centuries—and, once they had been civilized by Iranian culture or inspired by the Byzantine model, formed illustrious states and dynasties.

These nomads were not simply more or less permanent adversaries of the settled peoples with whom they maintained complex relations but they were also rivals and engaged in bitter internal fights. When one group triumphed over another, the latter would flee and push aside a third to secure for itself an area for grazing. The steppe was thus shaken by chain reactions that had repercussions on the periphery. Such was the case with Attila whose drive had the effect of precipitating the final onslaught of the Germans against Rome.

***

All the great civilizations were settled and urban: Mesopotamia and the Nile, the Yellow River, the Indus, the oasis-cities of Iran and the Mediterranean world; all had to endure the shocks of invasions by nomads. Today, the nomadic societies of High Asia are everywhere defeated, sedentarized, overtaken and controlled, but every civilization of the ancient and medieval world feared them.

As early as the sixth century B.C., according to Herodotus, the Achaemenid ruler Darius failed in 512 B.C. to deal a decisive blow to the Scythians, despite his military power: the Scythians practiced a scorched earth policy and retreated with nothing that could be seized except what they carried with them.

As for Rome, long before Attila, it came to know the manner of fighting of the mounted archers from central Asia in Cassius's disastrous encounter with the Parthians, recorded by Plutarch (battle of Carrhae, 53 B.C.).

As early as the fourth and third centuries B.C., China in the time of the "Warring Kingdoms" had to face raids by the Hsiung-Nu (Turkic-Mongols), and it was at that period that the first stretches were built of what was to become, when completed by the Ming, the Great Wall of China. Northern China was invaded and occupied in the fourth century A.D. by dynasties of nomad origin; again, from the tenth to the thirteenth centuries, culminating in the complete domination of the country by the Mongols in the thirteenth-fourteenth centuries; and then by the Manchus after 1644. For two millennia, the focus of Chinese foreign policy, with its periods of counter-offensives under the Han, the T'ang, the early Ming, and the Manchus once they had become sinicized, was on the threat from the nomads and, consequently, on controlling access routes to the west and its string of oases.

The Gupta dynasty in India, one of the greatest Indian dynasties, collapsed in the fifth century A.D. under attacks by the Hephthalite Huns (White Huns) who ravaged Iran as they passed through. The sultanate of Delhi, founded in the eleventh century by a dynasty of Turkic origin, was succeeded in the sixteenth century by Babur, a Turkic-speaking Chaghatai driven out of central Asia by the Uzbeks, who set off from Kabul to conquer India. He was a classic example of the deadly interplay of the chain reactions of nomad drives in which one group drove out another which, in turn, pushed aside a less powerful third one.

In Antiquity and the Middle Ages, China, which has always been highly adept at sinicizing Barbarian conquerors, Iran, and the Byzantine empire were the great centers civilizing the nomads of High Asia. The nomadic waves that penetrated into their orbit became transformed there, learned to govern states and ended up being converted to the religions of the settled peoples: Islam for the majority of them, or Buddhism.

China had the advantage—in addition to its culture—of numbers, which meant, that even if defeated, it was invulnerable. Iran, despite numerous intrusions from the north-east, succeeded in retaining its specific character, once it had adopted the Islam imposed by the Arab conquest, and its language and culture affected all those nomads whom it civilized and converted over an area stretching from central Asia to northern India.

The Byzantine empire survived the Roman empire in the West by a thousand years, and, among its many achievements, it successfully resisted the Goths, the Avars, the Arabs, the Bulgars, the Russians, the Pechenegs, and the Cumans.[2] These mounted a continuous succession of offensive pressures from south, north, east, and west until the final blow was delivered by the Ottomans once Constantinople was demographically squeezed. The Byzantine empire evangelized the Bulgars and Kievan Russia and also provided a state model for the Ottomans.

From the fifth to the thirteenth centuries, Europe in the broad sense also experienced the incursions and invasions of the Huns, the Avars, the Bulgars, the Magyars, the Pechenegs, the Cumans, and the Mongols. The latter's domination of Russia was peculiarly burdensome. As for the Ottoman drive in the fourteenth century from Asia Minor into the Balkans, it was, even before the fall of Constantinople in 1453, the final onslaught from central Asia started by the flight of a Turkic-speaking tribe driven out by the sudden upsurge of the Mongols at the beginning of the thirteenth century.

Western Europe, west of a line from Danzig through Vienna to Trieste, was the part of the medieval world best protected from nomad onslaughts, which doubtless explains why we are so little interested in central Asia. That is, of course, not true of the Hungarians whose plains from time immemorial served as the final resting place for nomadic waves from Asia. It is surely highly likely that the fact of having been spared Mongol and Ottoman rule contributed to the growth of Western Europe and promoted the preconditions for its exceptional destiny.

***

The warrior nomads lived along the northern fringes of the world of settled peoples. They traded their horses for products that they needed, such as textiles, or other luxury goods. The empires, whether Chinese or Byzantine, sought to divide them, pacify them, or contain them with tributes paid in the guise of gifts or alliances sealed by the marriage of an imperial princess with a Barbarian leader. And then, taking advantage of the weakening or strengthening of one of the antagonists, there would be an upsurge by the nomads or a punitive expedition or general offensive by the settled peoples.

Yet the nomads did not simply play a destabilizing role. Sometimes, after being civilized by settled peoples, they would contribute to a new stabilization. They, in turn, would found a dynasty. Among the most famous were the Yüan, founded by Kubilai Khan, which reigned for almost a century over the whole of China; the Seljukids, Iranized Turks who dominated much of the Middle East in the eleventh and twelfth centuries; the house of Osman (1299-1326), of lowly origin, which gradually became the formidable Ottoman empire; the Great Mughals founded by Babur, the conqueror of India (1526); and the Manchus who reigned over China for over two and a half centuries (1644-1911).

Other nomads formed empires in High Asia itself, like the Tuchueh, Turkic-speakers who ruled the area from the Caspian to Mongolia. These empires almost always broke up in one or two or at most three generations. But the Mongols fared better by dominating both central Eurasia and all of the periphery for a considerable period: China, the Iranian Middle East, Russia, and even parts of southeast Asia. With the Mongols, the mounted archers of central Asia reached their fullest development: throughout history they had used the same modes of combat, the same way of waging war which they carried to perfection: mobility, capacity to maneuver, impeccable logistics. Winter cost so many invaders of Russia dearly, but it proved for the Mongols to be highly favorable: the frozen rivers were easily crossed on horseback and the harshness of the winter was familiar to the sons of the steppe. It was on the contrary the mud of the spring thaw that saved the city of Novgorod. The thirteenth-century Mongols' discipline gave them a cohesion unequaled in the long line of steppe nomads.

In terms of population, Turkic-speaking nomads were the most numerous both in central Asia and beyond, once their Islamized descendants had been civilized by Persian culture or Byzantine influence, and their role was of enormous importance. They were to be found on every theater of conflict in the ancient and especially the medieval world: China, India, Iran, Syria, Egypt, Asia Minor, the Balkans. Timur

(Tamerlane), undeniably a military genius, attempted to repeat the formation of the world empire that Genghis Khan had achieved.

The decline of the nomads and their heirs accelerated in the mid-sixteenth century with the counter-offensive launched by Ivan the Terrible. But the khanate of the Crimea, sustained by the Ottomans, continued to be a threat throughout the seventeenth century and was only annexed in 1783, after two centuries in which the Cossacks and Russian settlers fought with them for the 1,200 kilometers that separated the Moscow of Ivan the Terrible from the Russia of Peter the Great and Catherine II. It was also in the mid-seventeenth century that the Manchus imposed their dynasty on the imperial throne of China.

Although from the sixteenth century onwards the history of High Asia tends to be of no more than regional significance, the nomads continued to be a formidable military force until the middle of the eighteenth century, when the use of artillery became decisive. In the last two centuries, the two countries that in the past most suffered from the nomads, Russia and China, have systematically put an end to the independence and nomadism of the mounted archers of whom the world once stood in such fear.

Nomads and Settled Peoples

Nomad comes from *nomas* (wandering shepherd). The Chinese used to say of the nomads: "They follow water and grass." That is a perfect definition of the pastoral world of the steppes of central Asia. Pastoralism in High Asia has always been based chiefly on horse and sheep, and to a lesser extent on cattle, goats, and camels.

Sheep provided the wool used for the felt of tents; the skin was used to make winter clothes; milk from the ewe was made into cheese; the sheep's flesh was eaten; and finally, its droppings were used as fuel. The horse was at once a means of transport, an instrument of war and hunting and a currency for trade. These were the hardy, thickset horses of the steppe that settled peoples wanted to obtain. The Chinese, for example, traded them for silk, tea, and grains. Mare's milk provided a favorite drink: *koumiss*. In case of need, if he had no other food, the nomad would drink a little of his horse's blood. Oxen and cows were draught animals. They hauled wagons on which yurts that had not been dismantled had been placed. The Bactrian camel was used particularly in desert regions.

The grazing circuit was determined by climatic conditions: semi-annual migrations between high pastures and lower level steppes. In winter, the uplands were deserted; in summer, the plains were dried out. Nomads moved over vast distances when circumstances required.

High Asia extends from the forests of Manchuria to the Black Sea and beyond, as far as the Hungarian *pustza*—the final outpost of the steppe. This region's center of gravity lay between the Kerulen, Orkhon, and Selenga rivers, north of modern Mongolia and south of Lake Baikal, the original home of the Turkic-Mongols, from where they attacked first China, then the world of Iran, India, Byzantium, and the Slavs. The Tungus-Manchus lived further east.

From east to west, this grassy steppe, bordered on the north by the Siberian forest, encounters no obstacle. All that is needed is to avoid the low marshy lands of western Siberia. Spring is the best season and the meadows are thick with grass and flowers; as the summer advances the grass dries out. Over more than ten thousand kilometers the continental climate is particularly harsh. In Urga, in Mongolia, the temperature varies, according to the season, between +35° and -40°, with frequent icy winds. In the south, the steppe ends at broken but very high mountain ranges, from the Caucasus to the Altai and including the Hindu Kush and the Pamirs, and at deserts, of which the most terrible are the Taklamakan and the Gobi. A few oases in the irrigated regions break the monotony of the landscape: those of the Ferghana and the Tarim basin, the central point in High Asia, oases along the so-called silk road with their famous names: Yarkend, Kashgar, Turfan, etc.

The conflict between nomads and settled peoples is the most long-standing conflict in the world and nowhere is this better illustrated than in central Asia.

These men of the steppe, whose origins lay in the forests, exceptionally frugal horsemen, shepherds having to subsist on little and often having to fight for the areas over which they roamed, were great conquerors and soldiers who without doubt rank among the most remarkable that the world has seen.

As early as the sixth century B.C., Darius came up against the defensive scorched earth strategy designed to provoke the collapse of an adversary too far from his logistical bases. In the first century B.C., the Roman legions rashly led by Crassus into the Syrian desert suffered a disaster at Carrhae, before the fighting strategy of the Parthians that came straight out of nomadic techniques.

After drawing the Romans onto unfavorable ground, far from help, the Parthians appeared. The legions awaited the shock; but, instead of that, writes Plutarch,

> They gave back, making as though they fled, and dispersed themselves. But the Romans marvelled when they found it contrary, and that it was but a device to environ them on every side. Whereupon Crassus commanded his shot and light armed men to assail them, the which they did: but they went not far, they were so beaten in with arrows, and driven to retire to their force of armed men. And this was the first beginning that both feared and troubled the Romans, when they saw the vehemency and great force of the enemies' shot, which brake their armours, and ran through anything they hit, were it never so hard or soft.

> The Parthians thus still drawing back, shot all together on every side, not aforehand, but at adventure: for the battle of the Romans stood so near together, as if they would, they could not miss the killing of some. These bowmen drew a great strength, and had big strong bows, which sent the arrows from them with a wonderful force. The Romans by means of these bows were in hard state. For if they kept their ranks, they were grievously wounded: again if they left them, and sought to run upon the Parthians to fight at hand with them, they saw they could do them but little hurt, and yet were very likely to take the greater harm themselves. For, as fast as the Romans came upon them, so fast did the Parthians fly from them, and yet in flying continued still their shooting: which no nation but the Scythians could better do than they, being a matter indeed most greatly to their advantage. For by their flight they best do save themselves, and fighting still, they thereby shun the shame of their flying.

> The Romans still defended themselves, and held it out, so long as they had any hope that the Parthians would leave fighting, when they had spent their arrows or would join battle with them. But after they understood that there were a great number of camels laden with quivers full of arrows, where the first that had bestowed their arrows fetched about to take new quivers: then Crassus seeing no end of their shot, began to faint, and sent to Publius his son, willing him in any case to charge upon the enemies, and to give an onset, before they were compassed in on every side. For it was on Publius' side, that one of the wings of the enemies' battle was nearest unto them, and where they rode up and down to compass them behind. Whereupon Crassus' son taking thirteen hundred horsemen with him (of the which, a thousand were of the men of arms whom Julius Caesar sent) and five hundred shot, with eight ensigns of footmen having targets, most near to the place where himself then was: he put them out in breadth, that wheeling about they might give a charge upon them that rode up and down. But they seeing him coming, turned straight their horse and fled...

> Publius Crassus seeing them fly, cried out, These men will not abide us, and so spurred on for life after them.... Now the horsemen of the Romans being trained out thus to the chase, their footmen also would not abide behind, nor show themselves to have less hope, joy and courage, than their horsemen had. For they thought all had been won, and that there was no more to do, but to follow the chase: till they were gone far from the army, and then they found the deceit. For the horsemen that fled before them, suddenly turned again, and a number of others besides came and set upon them. Whereupon they stayed, thinking that the enemies perceiving they were so few, would come and fight with them hand to hand.

Howbeit they set out against them their men at arms with their barbed horse, and made their light horsemen wheel around about them, keeping no order at all: who galloping up and down the plain, whirled up the sand hills from the bottom with their horse feet, which raised such a wonderful dust, that the Romans could scarce see or speak one to another. For they being shut up into a little room, and standing close to one another, were sore wounded with the Parthians' arrows, and died... Then [Publius] himself encouraging his horsemen, went and gave a charge, and did valiantly set upon the enemies, but it was with too great disadvantage, both for offence, and also for defence. For himself and his men with weak and light staves, brake upon them that were armed with curaces of steel, or stiff leather jacks. And the Parthians in contrary manner with mighty strong pikes gave charge upon these Gauls, which were either unarmed, or else but lightly armed...

And the most part of their horse were slain, charging with all their power upon the men at arms of the Parthians, and so ran themselves in upon the points of their pikes.

At the length, they were driven to retire towards their footmen, and Publius Crassus among them, who was very ill by reason of the wounds he had received. And seeing a sand hill by chance not far from them, they went thither, and setting their horse in the middest of it, compassed it in round with their targets, thinking by this means to cover and defend themselves the better from the barbarous people: howbeit they found it contrary. For the country being plain, they in the foremost ranks did somewhat cover them behind, but they that were behind, standing higher than they that stood foremost...could by no means save themselves, but were all hurt alike, as well the one as the other, bewailing their own misery and misfortune, that must needs die without revenge, or declaration of their valiancy."[3]

History has sometimes divided the steppe of High Asia into two: in the west, the plains of Ukraine, the northern Caucasus, and the Kirghiz and Kazakh steppes; in the east, Mongolia and Manchuria. But, in many ways, notably militarily, the steppe is one. The wolf, the *bestia senze pace* (beast without rest) as Konrad Lorenz calls it in his study of aggression, is the tutelary animal of every Turkic-Mongol group.

The image of the mounted archer, frequently reproduced both in Chinese painting and in Persian miniatures, is a clear indication of where the effectiveness of the warrior nomad lay: the horse, small, sturdy, wonderfully resistant to the cold of winter on the steppes and hardy since it could survive on grass alone if necessary; the double-curved bow was light and carried further than conventional bows. Used by the Scythians, Parthians, Huns, and Turkic-Mongols with terrible effectiveness arising from the fact that children were taught to use it from their earliest childhood and that the requirements of hunting made use of it an everyday affair, the bow was the nomad horseman's decisive weapon, enabling him to harass without taking the risk of frontal attack. This latter would only occur once the adversary had been weakened, thrown off balance, or disorientated by an assault by the heavy cavalry using lances, as with the Scythians, the two-sided broadsword as with the Huns, or the sword as with the Avars. The innovations to do with the horse—bit, reins, stirrup—or weaponry, such as the sword that would be universally adopted, from Japan to Western Europe through the intermediary of the Hungarians and Poles in contact with the Ottoman empire, are all inventions of the nomads. The arrow of the Parthian is the arrow of the Scythians and all who followed them. The decimal formation—perhaps inherited from the Achaemenids—was also common to all nomads: from the Huns to the Ottomans, the troops were organized into hundreds, thousands, and ten thousands, in disciplined formations.

When an energetic leader appeared capable of uniting the nomadic tribes and imposing a common discipline, methods of fighting and the conduct of war were refined, with the introduction of heavy cavalry, infantry, siege machines, etc., while retaining the qualities of mobility. This mobility was based on the lightness of the terrain, the number of re-mounts (three to five per horseman and sometimes more) and also on the steadiness of the men and horses of the steppe.

With time, there were alterations: a second bow was in use among the Mongols that was larger and had a greater range; the Arabian horse introduced through Transoxiana ended up supplanting all others (the lightest clothes were reserved for people of distinction). The infantry was sometimes transported on camel back. Elephants from India were used, notably by Tamerlane (as they had been by the Sassanids long before). Siege machines made their appearance: the Avars were the first to get their inspiration from Chinese equipment and took it with them as far as Europe. Boats were used on lakes and inland seas before the Mongols in the thirteenth century established a fleet for the conquest of Java and Japan.

Like the art of war, the habitat was also fundamentally the same from Mongolia to the Black Sea. The domain of the yurt stretched over ten thousand kilometers. The yurt is a cylindrical tent with a conical roof, and a lattice-work frame with roof battens made of willow or juniper lashed together by leather thongs; it is flexible and its insulation depends on layers of felt that give remarkable protection from the cold and wind. At the top of the roof, which remains open, a circular compression ring holds the poles and lets smoke out: it is called the "window on the sky," or the celestial eye from where light comes. The yurt's central column represents the pivot of the universe

***

The nomadic populations of High Asia had no linguistic unity in the sense of having a common language or common script, and in addition wrote very little: a few palaeo-Turkish inscriptions in the eighth century; the *Secret History of the Mongols*, a few scarce epics. But they shared the same magical-religious foundations based on belief in a supreme deity, Tengri, the Sky, and a host of minor gods. There were numerous rituals and prohibitions. Shamanism was widespread: it was the shaman who had the task of questioning the spirits and gods, interpreting the signs and curing the sick.

At the beginning of their imperial glory, the Mongols remained faithful to their beliefs and demonstrated exceptional tolerance of the religions that they encountered. But in their case, as happened with all the other peoples of the steppe, the great religions of the regions they occupied always ended up victorious. This was especially true of Islam, present in Transoxiana from the time of the Arab conquest but the religion of the large majority by the fourteenth century. It is likely that the collapse of Ming policy in High Asia in the fifteenth century and China's withdrawal behind the wall left the field free to Islam. Nestorian Christianity, widely propagated in centra Asia from the eighth century onward, had disappeared by the thirteenth century and given way to Islam. Mongolia alone embraced Buddhism in its Lamaist version.

The religious factor played a key role in the eyes of settled people in transforming nomads from Barbarians into civilized beings. Their conversion to Christianity, Islam, Manichaeism, or Buddhism gave them a status to which the nomads had previously been unable to aspire.

The image of these latter, such as it has come down to us from the historians is the same, whether it be the Chinese Ssu-ma Ch'ien on the Hsiung-nu, the Roman Ammianus Marcellinus on the Huns, or the Byzantine emperor Maurice on the Avars: "They are greedy, harsh, insatiable wolves."

But it would be a simplification to see the nomads as being always ready to pounce on the world of settled peoples and just waiting to rush to attack them. Most of the time, a fragile status quo prevailed where the two worlds met. Relations between settled peoples and nomads, of which Byzantium and China provide the most complete examples, were characterized by ever-changing relations of force. These might be based on trade in border markets, tributes paid by the state to nomads, or marriages symbolizing an often short-lived alliance, sometimes directed against another nomadic group. A change in that status quo—where, in Byzantium as in China, the trade in weapons with nomads remained forbidden—occurred when one of the parties felt that it had become more powerful. If this was the nomads, they could then demand a higher tribute or greater concessions. The state would usually give way, having no other choice. The turn to more extreme measures, as a result of this endless arm-twisting to extort more or give less, was signaled by a generalized assault by the nomads if they felt strong enough. Often these on-slaughts occurred when a dynasty was weakening. Conversely, under an energetic ruler, when the state was prosperous, the settled peoples would seek to drive the nomads back as far as possible by playing on their tribal dissensions or endeavoring to deprive them of their best support points. *The state never stopped moving from the use of diplomacy to the use of force; the nomads from the use of threatening neighborliness to deadly raiding, or even a generalized assault.*

The nomadic world was limited in terms of population, since hunting cannot feed a dense population. It was not numbers that enabled the nomads to succeed but *concentration* in attack, surprise, and an often very marked military superiority—with, facing them, dynasties that were often enfeebled and populations that were ill-prepared for the merciless manner of fighting of their nomadic adversaries.

Mutually profitable relations developed between nomads and settled peoples during periods of peace—although such periods remained dangerous. History written by settled peoples lays stress above all on the savagery of attacks by nomads. But the counter-attacks by settled peoples, whether China or Byzantium, were many and deadly.

The nomads' campaigns took place at the end of summer or the beginning of the autumn after the horses had been able to graze their fill and recover from the privations of winter. The settled peoples' campaigns, by contrast, took place at the beginning of spring when the adversary's cavalry was in a poor state.

In this relationship, always one of conflict whether that conflict was open or masked, the nomads often triumphed. But their triumph was always relatively short-lived. For the nomads to have victory for any lasting period, would require that they adopt the forms of management of the settled peoples, notably state forms. The dynasties of nomadic origin became urbanized, although they remained warlike and conquering. The religious ideology and culture of the settled peoples won in the end. The cultural depth of China or Iran withstood every assault, although some of those assaults were formidable. The Byzantine empire was able to survive a thousand years and bequeathed the Orthodox world as a legacy.

In the fifth century, India saw the glorious Gupta dynasty disappear under the blows of the Hephthalite Huns. Then it had the privilege of five centuries of respite. But from the tenth century onwards until the Mughal conquest and rule that ended only with the arrival of the British, it was indelibly marked by the domination imposed by Iranized and Islamized Turkic-speaking nomads.

Only Western Europe escaped the catastrophic consequences of the loss of urban liberties that Russia experienced with the Mongol conquest in the thirteenth century, followed by two and a half centuries of yoke. Western Europe, unlike the Balkans, was not marked by five centuries of Ottoman occupation (fourteenth-nineteenth centuries).

The Nomadic Model: The Scythians

The oldest nomadic warrior in central Eurasia is the Scythian. From the seventh century B.C. to the middle of the third century A.D., the Scythian presence made itself felt at the expense of numerous neighbors. The Scythians occupied the steppes between the Don and the Danube, to the west of the territory of the Sarmatians, who like them belonged to the Iranian linguistic group, and they left many archaeological remains. It is possible that they occupied these regions after, in accordance with one of the laws of the steppes, driving the Cimmerians out into Anatolia (eighth century B.C.).

We mainly know about the Scythians from Herodotus who recorded what he learned about them while he was visiting the Greek city of Olbia on the Bug-Dniestr estuary in the middle of the fifth century B.C. His story is largely corroborated by recent archaeological discoveries. Various Assyrian and Urartian royal inscriptions add to our knowledge, and the material culture of the Scythians is now quite well known.

The military presence of the Scythians is attested to in the countries of western Asia: Mesopotamia, Iran, Syria and beyond as far as

Egypt. In 612 B.C., the Scythians took part alongside the Babylonians and the Medes in the capture of Nineveh, which marked the destruction of the Assyrian empire. In the sixth century B.C., they were driven back north of the Caucasus by the Medes, but not before they had destroyed the stronghold of the capital of the kingdom of Urartu at Karmir Blur, near Yerevan (Armenia).

Towards the end of the sixth century, in 512 B.C., Darius, the third of the great Achaemenid kings, who is better known for having tried to bring down Athens, embarked on an expedition against the Scythians in order to put an end to their incursions and passed through Thrace and Bessarabia. As Herodotus records,

> While Darius was preparing his invasion of Scythia, and sending messengers to every part of his dominions with orders to raise troops here, ships there, and labourers somewhere else to work on the bridge over the Bosphorus...

> The Scythians, after discussing the situation and concluding that by themselves they were unequal to the task of coping with Darius in a straight fight, sent off messengers to their neighbours, whose chieftains had already met and were forming plans to deal with what was evidently a threat to their safety on a very large scale...

> Seeing that these nations refused to support them, they decided to avoid a straight fight, and to retire before the advance of the invader, blocking up all wells and springs which they passed on the march and stripping the country of all green stuff which might serve as forage. They organized their forces in two divisions, one of which...had orders to counter any movement the Persians might make by withdrawing along the coast of Lake Maeotis toward the river Tanais, and, should the Persians themselves retreat, to attack them in their turn.... [The second division was] to withdraw before the Persian advance at the distance of a day's march, and carry out as they went the same strategy of destroying the sources of supply. This second division was to begin by retiring in the direction of those nations who had refused to join the alliance, with the object of involving them in the war against their will—the idea being, if they would not fight on their own initiative, to force them into doing so.... The Scythians sent their best horsemen to reconnoitre in advance of the army. They themselves then marched out to meet Darius, and arranged for the waggons which served as houses for the women and children, and all the cattle, except what they needed for food, to move northward at once, in advance of their future line of retreat. The scouts made contact with the Persians about three days' march from the Danube, and at once encamped at a distance of a single day's march in front of them, destroying everything which the land produced. The Persians, on the appearance of the Scythian cavalry, gave chase and continued to follow in their tracks as they withdrew before them.... The Scythians crossed the river, and the Persians followed in pursuit, until they...reached [the territory] of the Budini, where they came across the wooden fortified town of Gelonus, abandoned and empty of defenders, and burnt it.... After burning the town, they continued to press forward on the enemies' heels until they reached the great uninhabited region which lies beyond the territory of the Budini. This tract of land is seven days' journey across...

When he reached this uninhabited area, Darius called a halt on the banks of the Oarus, and began to build eight large forts, spaced at regular intervals of about eight miles. The remains of them were still to be seen in my day. While these forts were under construction, the Scythians whom he had been following changed the direction of their march, and by a broad sweep through the country to the northward returned to Scythia and completely disappeared. Unable to see any sign of them, Darius left his forts half finished and himself turned back towards the west, supposing that the Scythians...were now trying to escape in that direction. He made the best speed he was capable of, and on reaching Scythia fell in with the other two combined divisions of the Scythian army; at once he gave chase, and they, as before, withdrew a day's march in front of him...

This ineffective and interminable chase was too much for Darius, who at last dispatched a rider with a message for Idanthyrsus, the Scythian king. "Why on earth, my good sir," the message ran, "do you keep on running away? You have, surely, a choice of two alternatives: if you think yourself strong enough to oppose me, stand up and fight, instead of wandering all over the world in your efforts to escape me; or, if you admit you are too weak, what is the good, even so, of running away? You should rather send earth and water to your master, as the sign of your submission, and come to a conference."

"You do not understand me, my lord of Persia," Idanthyrsus replied. "I have never yet run from any man in fear; nor do I do so now from you. There is, for me, nothing unusual in what I have been doing: it is precisely the sort of life I always lead, even in times of peace. If you want to know why I will not fight, I will tell you: in our country there are no towns and no cultivated lands; fear of losing a town or seeing crops destroyed might indeed provoke us to hasty battle—but we possess neither. If, however, you are determined upon bloodshed with the least possible delay, one thing there is for which we will fight—the tombs of our forefathers. Find those tombs, and try to wreck them, and you will soon know whether or not we are willing to stand up to you. Till then—unless the fancy takes us—we shall continue to avoid battle..."

Seeing the Persians disorganized by these continual raids, the Scythians hit upon a stratagem to keep them longer in the country and reduce them in the end to distress from lack of supplies. This was to slip away from time to time to some other district, leaving behind a few cattle in charge of shepherds; the Persians would come and take the animals, and be much encouraged by the momentary success. This happened time and again, until at last Darius did not know where to turn...[4]

The pursuit continued as far as the right bank of the Volga but was abandoned there, Darius' troops, already reduced in number, being exhausted. Darius withdrew as best he could as far as the Danube, without having had the chance to use his military resources against the Scythians who were using scorched earth tactics.

In 496 B.C., the Scythians invaded Thrace, which was then held by Persia. Almost continuously, all through the fifth century B.C., they raided all over south-western Asia: Syria, northern Persia, Anatolia. The Scythians were at their height in the fourth and third centuries B.C. At that time they were divided into two groups: one, far and away the largest, in the Crimea and Ukraine as far as the Dniepr, called the royal Scythians, the other in Bulgaria. This was also the time of their greatest cultural flowering. Numerous remains have been found in Ukraine and date from the fourth-third centuries B.C. Animal art is particularly striking among these hunters.

Apart from Herodotus, there are few written sources: Strabo (Book XI, chapter 11) mentions their presence in the Crimea and Polybius (XXXV, 1) regards them still as a power in 179 B.C.

At the end of the second century B.C., the Greek cities of the Crimea, along the Black Sea, were repeatedly sacked. The Chersonesus turned to Mithridates VI Eupator, king of Pontus, who defeated the Scythians in three hard-fought expeditions. But it was not long before they were once again upsetting the economic life of the Greek trading cities. It was only in A.D. 63 that the Roman general Platinius Silvanus finally succeeded in loosening the Scythian vice around the Chersonesus.

Driven back westward by the Sarmatians (second century), who were themselves being pressed upon by the Alans (ancestors of the Ossetians), it was only in the mid-third century A.D. that the Scythians were driven out of Ukraine and the Crimea by the Goths and ceased to exist after an existence of a thousand years.

Herodotus also shows us the military codes and values on which Scythian society rested—so typical of nomads or those who were labeled Barbarians:

As regards war, the Scythian custom is for every soldier to drink the blood of the first man he kills. The heads of all enemies killed in battle are taken to the king; a head being a sort of ticket by which a soldier is admitted to his share of the loot—no head, no loot. He strips the skin of the head by making a circular cut round the ears and shaking out the skull; he then scrapes the flesh off the skin with the rib of an ox, and when it is clean works it in his fingers until it is supple, and fit to be used as a sort of handkerchief. He hangs these handkerchiefs on the bridle of his horse, and is very proud of them. The finest fellow is the man who has the greatest number. Many Scythians sew a number of scalps together and make cloaks out of them, like the ones peasants wear, and often, too, they take the skin, nails and all, off the right hands and arms of dead enemies and use it to cover their quivers with.... Sometimes they flay the whole body, and stretch the skin on a wooden frame which they carry around with them when they ride. They have a special way of dealing with the actual skulls—not with all of them, but only those of their worst enemies: they saw off the part below the eyebrows, and after cleansing out what remains stretch a piece of rawhide round it on the outside...the skull is then used to drink from.... When important visitors arrive, these skulls are passed around, and the host tells the story of them...[5] Once a year the governor of each district mixes a bowl of wine, from which every Scythian who has killed his man in battle has the right to drink. Those who have no dead enemy to their credit are not allowed to touch the wine, but have to sit by themselves in disgrace—the worst, indeed, which they can suffer. Any man, on the contrary, who has killed a great many enemies, has two cups and drinks from both of them at once."[6]

Such behavior dictated by conditions in which there is no way of admitting a rival, is common to all the peoples of the steppe—although it is not peculiar to them. Harsh conditions determine behavior based on exaltation of physical courage, endurance and pitilessness.

Settled peoples were essentially concerned with relations between themselves and the nomads. But inter-nomad relations were just as deadly right from the very beginning. Grazing disputes, migration, drought, population growth, and the quest for power all drove nomadic groups, already deeply attached to tribal links and almost always regarding other groups, however close, as hostile, to confrontation. That is the source of those endless chain-reactions as one group pushed another, where groups fled in front of others or were absorbed or made sometimes short-lived submissions. Even before it became predatory on the settled world, the basic mechanism of nomadic life was self-destructive and pitilessly ferocious.

Notes

1. With the exception of René Grousset whose *L'Empire des steppes* (Paris: Payot, 1939) (*The Empire of the Steppes. A History of Central Asia,* trans. N. Walford (New Brunswick, NJ: Rutgers University Press, 1970) was a pioneering work. However, he was little interested in military problems or the geopolitical dimension.
2. A Turkic-speaking people like the Pechenegs, the Cumans were also known as Kipchaks or Polovtsis.
3. From "Crassus," in *Lives of the Noble Grecians and Romans*, ed. Paul Turner, trans. James Amyot and Thomas North (Carbondale: Southern Illinois University Press, 1963), I, 268-272.
4. *Herodotus. The Histories*, Book IV, trans. and with an introduction by Aubrey de Selincourt (Harmondsworth: Penguin Books, 1954).
5. Samuel Cosman Papers, U. S. Marine Corps Historical Center, Washington, D. C. as cited in P. Fussell, *Wartime. Understanding and Behavior in the Second World War* (New York: Oxford University Press, 1989). The skulls of Japanese were cleaned and kept as trophies during the Second World War in the Pacific. "This treatment of Japanese corpses as if they were animal became so flagrant as early as September 1942, that the Commander in Chief of the Pacific Fleet ordered that 'No part of the enemy's body may be used as a souvenir...'"
6. *Herodotus. The Histories*, Book IV.

2

The Military Fronts of the Altaic Nomads (Fourth Century B.C.-Twelfth Century A.D.)

The military fronts of the Altaic nomads covered the whole area, apart from the Maghrib, where the conflicts of the ancient and medieval world unfolded. Over the two thousand years during which these nomads exerted their pressure, they were twice involved in events of world importance: in the fourth and fifth centuries and in the thirteenth, fourteenth, and fifteenth centuries A.D., the first time through a series of invasions that directly precipitated the fall of the Han empire in China and the Gupta empire in India and indirectly that of the Roman empire, and the second, which came as the climax of three centuries of upheavals precipitated by nomads from Turkestan in the Middle East, was the work of Genghis Khan and his Mongol successors who built the largest empire the world has ever seen.

But, apart from these great invasions going off in all directions, throughout those two thousand years the various peoples of High Asia were continually harassing settled societies, or, whenever they could, taking them over or, on the contrary, sometimes having to endure counter-attacks by them.

Given the original homeland of these peoples, in present-day Mongolia in the case of the Turkic-Mongols and in Manchuria, the prime objective of the nomads, from the fourth century B.C. to the middle of the seventeenth century A.D., was China: through those two thousand years, the chief focus of China's external policy was its conflictual relations with the nomads.

On several occasions, northern China was conquered by nomads whose dynasties rapidly became sinicized before they were themselves submerged by other waves of nomads who, in turn, became sinicized. Three times the Chinese empire counter-attacked, very vigorously under the Han and the T'ang, and in a less sustained manner under the Ming, who, in the end, opted for isolation. Twice China was wholly conquered, first by the Mongols and then by the Manchus who, once sinicized, resumed China's traditional policy towards the nomads of endeavoring to control the route through the oases as far north-eastward as possible in order to keep the nomads as far away as possible.

All through the first millennium A.D., the nomad drive, by the Turkic-speakers in particular, was from east to west, and by the eleventh century numbers were making it irresistible on the Iranian front. From Transoxiana, which had de facto become a Turkestan, Turkic-speaking tribes occupied the area where Iranian civilization predominated, that is as far as Afghanistan and the Punjab.

Like China, although to a lesser extent for demographic reasons, Iran was at once a civilizing and an integrating force. *In the ancient and medieval world Iran was one of the great matrices of human history.*

The Seljukids, like the Ghaznids, benefited from Persian learning in many ways, and the adoption of Islam brought these Iranized former nomads into the embrace of civilization. By the eleventh century, the Byzantine empire was suffering seriously from the pressure of the Turkic-speakers but, nevertheless, managed to survive until the middle of the fifteenth century when the Ottomans administered the coup de grâce. In the previous century, the Ottomans had conquered the Balkans and occupied the western part of Anatolia, thereby placing a demographic stranglehold on an empire, which had been moribund since the thirteenth century and was soon no more than a city under siege.

Meanwhile, in the mid-thirteenth century, slave soldiers, mostly Turkic-speaking, who were serving the Mamluks in Egypt, seized power, and showed their skills in combat against the Mongols and the Crusaders.

Russia's fate was indeed a singular one, seeking refuge from the nomads, as it were, in the twelfth century, by abandoning the steppe around Kiev for the northern forests and, a century later, succumbing almost totally for a long period to the Mongol yoke. It was not until Ivan the Terrible that the Russian counter-offensive began to get under way in the second half of the sixteenth century. And it was only really completed when Peter the Great and after him Catherine II had subdued and then eliminated the khanate of the Crimea. Meanwhile, it took two centuries of stubborn, inch by inch advance to win the twelve hundred kilometers that separated Moscow from the Sea of Azov.

While, until the thirteenth century, Hungary and its grazing lands were at once the terminus of the nomad waves and their refuge, the Balkans were subjected to the newly forming Ottoman empire in the second half of the fourteenth century. Western Europe has the privilege of not having experienced any external invasion since the middle of the tenth century. That makes it a unique case, along with Japan, it, too, saved from the Mongol tempest, like the European West, by the effect of a fortunate stroke of circumstance.

Nowhere, outside the steppe, did the revolution that the use of cavalry represented have such military effectiveness. Mobility, capacity of concentration, the range and power of penetration of the double-curved bow, techniques of harassment and feints made the nomads of the steppe the major representative of a strategic culture of an exceptional effectiveness in which warfare was a natural extension of the hunt whose prey had ceased to be animals, a situation that lasted until the advent of forearms.

The Chinese Front

Throughout its history, for over two thousand years, China had to guard itself in the north against nomad invasions, launch, when it had the means to do so, vast counter-offensives to ensure its control of the steppes through the oases of central Asia or suffer partial, and, on two occasions total, occupation, by nomads.

As early as the time of the "Warring Kingdoms" (fourth century B.C.), if not before, the chronicles mention nomad invasions. Under the Chin dynasty (Qin, 221-207 B.C.), a system of walls was erected in the north. From the end of the third century B.C. to the second century A.D., the Hsiung-nu nomads (Turkic-Mongols) appeared as a fearsome power posing what was virtually a standing threat, except in the periods when the Han dynasty (206 B.C.-A.D. 220) took the offensive and made itself mistress of central Asia as far as present-day Uzbekistan.

According to the great Chinese historian Ssu-ma Ch'ien (145-87 B.C.), it was during the reign of Wu Ling (325-298 B.C.), ruler of the northern Chinese state of Chao, that, in order to put up an effective resistance to the incursions of the Hsiung-nu, the Chinese transformed their chariot-mounted troops into cavalry in order to gain mobility.

They also gave up wearing their long robe and replaced it with the nomad trousers, which were better suited to horse-riding and set about forming corps of mounted archers. Under the same emperor, new walls were built as an obstacle at the most vulnerable points. By the beginning of the third century, other northern Chinese states, Yen and Ch'in, were also building walls in southern Manchuria.

The Chinese chronicles inform us that the Hsiung-nu were often of what we would call Mongolian appearance, but among them were to be found warriors with light-colored mustaches and blue eyes. They wore fur caps, wide trousers tied at the ankles by straps, a loose dress hanging half way down their thighs, slit on the sides, a short fur cloak and leather shoes. They wore rings in their ears. They ate mainly meat and milk, slept in tents and had a cult of *Tengri*, "the Sky god," with whom shamans would intercede. Ssu-ma Ch'ien comments, "Boys begin by learning to herd sheep, trap rats and birds and ride horses."

Han China

Near the middle of its course, the Yellow River makes a great bend northward. This area is known as the Ordos. Control of the Ordos is strategically vital if northern China is to be protected. Under the first Han emperor, civil disturbances drove a host of Chinese who had recently been settled there to guard the frontier southward (210 B.C.). This vacuum at once attracted the Hsiung-nu nomads who seized the Ordos just at the point when they had equipped themselves with an outstanding leader: Motun.

The biography of this latter as it is recorded by Ssu-ma Ch'ien (chapter 110 of the *Records of the Historian* or *Shi ji*) is a splendid evocation that conveys the character of an archetypical type of steppe leader:

> Motun was one of the sons of Tumen, the chieftain of the Hsiung-nu. His father preferred one of his other sons and sent Motun as hostage to a rival tribe, the Yüeh-chih, and then attacked them, which logically ought to have meant that Motun would be put to death. But he managed to scramble on to a horse and escaped and returned home. The Hsiung-nu regarded him as a hero, and his father put him in command of 10,000 cavalry whom he drilled in his own way. Whenever he shot an arrow, they had to aim at the same target, whatever it might be. After drilling them like that, one fine day while they were hunting he aimed an arrow at his own favourite horse and put to death all those who failed to follow his example. On another occasion, he shot at one of his father's favourite concubines. All the men did likewise. Feeling that they were now suitably disciplined, one day when he was out hunting with his father, he shot an arrow at him; his men did likewise, thus sharing in his crime, and Motun proclaimed himself the new *Shan-yü*.

After defeating two rival tribes, Motun turned against China and occupied the Ordos. That was in 209 B.C. Eight years later, the Han decided to counter-attack. But in vain. One of the four Chinese generals went over to the enemy or was suspected of treachery. Dynastic loyalties were unsure. And the emperor himself suffered a disaster while on a punitive expedition and only just managed to escape. The nomads had a clear military superiority. China drew the consequences. A treaty was soon signed between the Han and the nomads (198 B.C.). A Chinese princess became one of the wives of the *Shan-yü* (a chiefly title) Motun and the Chinese undertook to deliver grain, silk, and alcohol at regular intervals. In return, the Hsiung-nu undertook not to invade China. When the nomads had grown stronger, their ruler, who declared himself "the great *Shan-yü* [paramount chief] of the Hsiung-nu mandated by heaven," in the Chinese manner, demanded that the treaty be renegotiated on even more advantageous terms. Meanwhile, the Hsiung-nu had established their hegemony over the steppe. They drove the Yüeh-chih out of Kansu, and the Yüeh-chih migrated towards Bactriana (76 B.C.). The *Shan-yü* who succeeded Motun (174 B.C.) launched two incursions: the first into Chen Si (167 B.C.), the second a year later into Kansu, and he secured a new treaty. Again, the next *Shan-yü* did not honor the terms of the treaty and invaded northern China (158 B.C.).

In fact, each new nomad ruler asserted his power by conducting victorious military operations in order to tilt the balance of forces to his advantage and thus obtain a new treaty on more advantageous terms than the previous one. The Hsiung-nu's military operations were successful not only because of the superiority of the nomad mounted archers but also because, each time, it was the latter who took the initiative and so had the advantage of surprise and the power of concentration their mobility gave them. Thus, in the space of just sixty years (198-135 B.C.), the Han and the nomads negotiated more than ten treaties by which the latter extracted concessions each time: an increase in the number of deliveries of goods which were, in fact, a tribute but which the empire, in order not to lose face, preferred to regard as "gifts," or an increase in the number of licenses to trade at border posts. The incursions became less frequent by the end of the period mentioned and there were only two in twenty years (144 and 142 B.C.). This precarious neither peace nor war situation was costly, but apparently doomed to go on forever. The Han built more and more stretches of wall or sought an ally in the nomads' rear or went on the attack. No strategy seemed able to put an end to nomad pressure: not the illusory one of locking themselves up behind walls, not treaties of neutrality, not even an alliance in the rear, not, in the long run, offensives. The relations of force were changing all the time. And the nomads were still just as threatening. But when a dynasty was strong, an offensive was the most tempting prospect. This is what happened on several occasions in the course of Chinese history. The prime aim of the Chinese was to win back control of the Ordos, the strategic bend in the Yellow River, the possession of which enabled the nomads to ravage northern China at will or seize whatever city happened to be the capital. For about half of Chinese history, the Ordos was controlled by nomads who thus made a permanent threat hang over northern China which they dominated for lengthy periods on several occasions.

Ssu-ma Ch'ien records the mission of Chang Ch'ien (c. 140 B.C.), the Han emperor's emissary to the west, in order to make an alliance in the rear with the Yüeh-chih against the Hsiung-nu—the former having every reason to seek revenge against the latter.[1] But Chang Ch'ien was captured by the Hsiung-nu on the way. He lived among them for ten years, married there but was able to make his escape. He continued his journey to Turkestan and failed to conclude an alliance; the Yüeh-chih, who are identified with the Kushans (Indo-Europeans), were not interested.[2] On the way home he was again captured, again escaped and got back to China thirteen years after he had left, with his wife and the guide of an expedition that had initially comprised a hundred-strong escort. The knowledge amassed by Chang Ch'ien about the culture of the nomads, their strengths and their weaknesses, was invaluable, and he participated as an adviser in the first Han military counter-offensives. Before long he was again being sent on a mission to the west (115 B.C.) where he made abortive contacts with Ferghana and Sogdiana at a time when Han policy aimed at nothing less than "cutting off the nomads' right arm," that is driving them back north of the desert. But these expeditions were particularly costly in horses and difficult logistically for the Chinese, and could not last too long. No campaign lasted more than three months, most being of shorter duration. But the signal had been given. Having driven the nomads back northward, the Han now sought to extend their control westward, into the regions that provided the bulk of the nomads' subsistence. Once the Ordos was held, what counted in terms of strategy to weaken the nomads was control of the routes north and south of the Tian Shan and the Kansu corridor. Cut off from these vital areas, the nomads were driven towards the northern steppes and forest areas.

Pursuing their offensive, the Han reached Ferghana (101 B.C.) and gradually asserted their control over the string of oases along what is known as the silk road. They thus succeeded in decisively strengthening their situation by controlling the western regions and investing the territories bordering on the Tian Shan (Celestial mountains). The Hsiung-nu were forced not only to retreat northward, thus losing sources of supply, but also to abandon the duties they imposed all along the route through the oases. Their defeats also, classically, precipitated an uprising by the tribes and peoples they had been holding down. The Han dominated central Asia as far as present-day Uzbekistan. A protectorate over the western regions was established and military colonies began to be introduced, each colony having some 500 soldier-farmers and their wives. These colonies were easily made in the oases with their carefully regulated agriculture, close to what the Chinese peasant was used to.

The Han had been able to respond to the nomad incursions so long crowned with success by *adapting*. In the reign of the emperor Wu-ti (140-87 B.C.), in the space of a few decades, the Han turned the situation around by controlling the oases of High Asia. The Ordos, now retaken, was settled—according to the Chronicles—by 100,000 Chinese (127 B.C.). Whatever the figure, the fact is that the Ordos became Chinese at this date, even though it was frequently dominated by nomad waves over the fifteen centuries that followed.

The walls that Shih-huang-ti (Qin Shi, 247-210 B.C.), the creator of the Chinese empire, had built were very patchy, and linked or strengthened stretches built by other dynasties, but proved to be totally inadequate every time there was a large-scale incursion. Subsequently, the Northern Ch'i, the Sui and above all the Ming built other stretches. The famous Great Wall of China, as a continuous construction, is the work of the Ming (1368-1644) starting in the middle of the fifteenth century, when they abandoned a policy of overland expansion—just as they abandoned the exploratory maritime expeditions that had taken Chinese fleets to the coasts of Africa at the beginning of the fifteenth century.

But when it was possible, an offensive policy showed itself to be much more effective than a policy of seclusion. A second defeat was inflicted on the nomads (121 B.C.) thanks to the use of a well-trained light cavalry, which was quite the equal of that of the nomads. The Hsiung-nu were driven back northward. Two Chinese generals, long used to border warfare and highly familiar with the nomad world, launched a victorious offensive and pursued the *Shan-yü* as far as the area of Lake Baikal (119 B.C.). The Hsiung-nu abandoned their capital south of the Gobi and transferred it further north. On the borders, in the contact zones, military commanders gradually adapted to the reality of the strategic culture and manner of fighting of the adversary: a light cavalry of archers capable of harassing the enemy or blocking them on their own ground was formed; a heavy cavalry designed for shock, equipped with good horses in adequate numbers was strengthened; the train was lightened, etc. Thanks to a state with resources and maintaining a sustained policy, when they were at their height, the Han succeeded in realizing the geopolitical aim of every Chinese dynasty that had been able to conduct a power policy: dominating the area north and west of China properly so-called and above all reaching out towards the oases along the silk road, Zungharia, the Tarim basin, and Chinese Turkestan. Under the T'ang and more ephemerally under the Ming, imperial China resumed the same policy towards the western regions. Once sinicized, the Manchu dynasty pursued the same aims (as did revolutionary China). For over two thousand years of conflicts with the nomads, China succeeded in dominating the area along the oases of central Asia almost one quarter of the time.

As often happens when the wind shifts and setbacks accumulate, internal disputes erupted among the Hsiung-nu and the idea of making neighborly concessions—even acknowledging Chinese pre-eminence—began to be heard. One of the sons of the Shan-yü was sent as a hostage (53 B.C.) and, two years later, the leader of the Hsiung-nu presented himself at the imperial court to pay homage. Soon a treaty of alliance was signed (43 B.C.). The Han provided military assistance to the Hsiung-nu against other nomads who seemed to be getting stronger (the Chih-Chih[3]). With Han troops and Hsiung-nu contingents, a Chinese general defeated the Chih-Chih nomads (36 B.C.), and the Hsiung-nu, who had since their weakening become in a way "federated," retained cordial relations with the Han for almost half a century.

During the first century A.D., the Hsiung-nu split between those in the north, hostile to China, and those in the south, on the marches of the empire, who remained under Han protection. The Chinese, playing on nomad divisions, launched four offensives against the Northern Hsiung-nu in the space of twenty years (73-91) and were successful each time. In addition, the Hsien-pi, from the upper Amur inflicted a heavy defeat on the Hsiung-nu in 96. It was not until the Chinese weakened in the second century in the face of a whole series of crises, that the Hsiung-nu made a return offensive (107 and 123) trying to free the Tarim basin and invest southern Mongolia.

As the first millennium began, Han China was, along with Rome, Gupta India, the Parthians, and the Kushan empire, one of the five imperial powers of the time. But its decline was already under way.

After the Han

When the Han dynasty disappeared amid civil war (220), it was replaced by the "Three Kingdoms," but the nomads continued to be submissive. Those who attempted an incursion were driven back. Along the marches there remained the Southern Hsiung-nu who, for two centuries, had been subject to the influence of Chinese culture. In 317, the Shan-yü of the Southern Hsiung-nu, initiating a process that would be repeated again and again in Chinese history, overthrew the Ch'in dynasty and founded the first, short-lived, non-Chinese dynasty, which called itself "Latter Han."

The whole of the north was soon occupied, including the capitals of Ch'ang-an and Lo-yang. One member of the imperial family took refuge in Nankin (Chien-k'ang) and, in the shelter of the Blue River, founded a second Ch'in dynasty, known as the Southern Ch'in (Jin) dynasty. For three centuries (317-589), Nankin replaced Chang-an and Lo-yang as the imperial capital.

While the properly Chinese dynasty reigned in the south, a succession of ephemeral hordes burst into the north from the fourth century onwards, among which only the T'o-pa (Tabgach) stand out. They succeeded in creating a northern state known as the Wei kingdom (386-534). Just before the creation of the Wei dynasty, the emperor Fu Chien (357-385) was a protector of Buddhism, and he also undertook to unify the northern states and launch an offensive to reconquer central Asia as far as Turfan. The Wei seized Lo-yang (422), the northern capital, and rapidly became sinicized. By the middle of the fifth century the Wei dominated all the northern kingdoms, adopted Buddhism and made themselves the defenders of Chinese civilization. At the end of the century, Wei China created the masterpieces of Buddhist art at Long Men. After ruling for a hundred and fifty years the dynasty collapsed (534), riven by internal divisions. An energetic warrior, Sui Wen-ti (581-604) succeeded in reunifying China (589) after a long period of fragmentation.

It was a process that was classic in China, as the nomad victor, long in contact with Chinese culture became sinicized, was followed by a new nomad wave that swept aside the sinicized dynasty whose warrior virtues had been softened with time. As for Chinese history, as Owen Lattimore characterizes it,[4] it seems to follow a recurrent pattern: after an extended period of war and upheavals, a dynasty appears which puts an end to nomad invasions and peasant rebellions. Peace is restored with whatever harshness is required. The dynasty then experiences a period of greater or lesser prosperity that lasts a varying time. Gradually, the administration becomes corrupt and weak, while heavily taxing the impoverished and discontented peasantry. The last emperor of the dynasty is often incapable. Power struggles erupt in a climate of civil war, while nomad pressures intensify.

This description may be a little schematic, but it is true that every dynasty that was founded by conquering nomads was able to impose itself because the properly Chinese dynasties of the time were weakened. Such was the case in the eleventh century with the Khitans, in the twelfth century with the Jurchens, and in the seventeenth century with the Manchus.

In northern Wei China, the Juan-juan (a proto-Mongol group) had formed a threatening nomad empire in the steppe (402), but the Wei were able to contain them for over a century. They built a new wall some two thousand kilometers long. They even launched two major offensives against the nomads north of the Gobi (443 and 449). Each time, following a tactic already used by the Scythians, the nomads melted away. The Wei troops advanced as far as the Orkhon, but the cold hurt them severely. However, ten years later, the Wei managed to win a decisive victory (458). But the weakened Juan-juan retained hegemony over the steppe until the middle of the sixth century.

Like many nomad governments, that of the Juan-juan collapsed as a result of both internal divisions and external attacks. The Wei and the Tu-chueh, supposedly allies, fought each other. The Tu-chueh were proto-Turks, and so called in the Chinese chronicles. They built an empire (552) which for a generation embraced the whole of High Asia. The language used by the dynasty was Sogdian (an Indo-European language).

By about the mid-sixth century, the steppe was shared among three groups: the Juan-juan, who dominated the area between Manchuria and Turfan; the Hephthalite Huns, who ruled over Turkestan, Afghanistan, eastern Iran, and as far as the Punjab; and finally, the Black Huns, who, after terrorizing the Roman empire in the time of Attila a century earlier, were now weakened and divided, and roamed the Ukrainian and Russian steppe.

The Tu-chueh, whose totem according to the Chinese chronicles was the wolf, had been not only the vassals of the Juan-juan but their weapon makers. Taking advantage of a conflict between the Juan-juan and the Wei, the Tu-chueh took them in a pincer movement and crushed them. The Juan-juan withdrew westward. The Tu-chueh empire was short-lived (552-583), and split into the Western Tu-chueh (583-657) and the Eastern Tu-chueh (583-630). But, by about 570, the presence of the Tu-chueh was making itself felt from Byzantium to China. They allied with the Sassanids, annihilated the Hephthalite Huns, and carved up Bactria and Sogdiana as well as Iran between them. The capital of the empire was on the Orkhon, and it was there that the khaghan reigned—a title borrowed from the Juan-juan.

The Chinese chronicles say: "They live in felt tents. They raise herds and they hunt. Their officers are hereditary. Their weapons: the bow and arrows that whistle. The spear and the sword. At the top of their flag-pole: a wolf's head.... Dying in battle is a matter of pride and they would blush with shame to die of an illness." They also say: "The Tu-chueh are not even one percent of the Chinese. They seek out water and grazing lands, engage in hunting, do not have fixed homes and glory in war. When they feel themselves strong, they go on the attack. If they believe themselves weak, they flee and hide themselves. They thus make up for the advantage in numbers that the Chinese have and which does not help the latter at all." The Byzantine chronicler Theophylact Simocattes mentions: "These nomads worship fire, honour air and water and call the creator of the sky and the earth 'Tengri'." Firdusi's *Shah Nameh*—the great Persian national epic written in the tenth century—has references to the struggles between the Sassanids and their Turanian (Turkish) neighbors. The Western Tu-chueh formed an alliance with Byzantium, ever anxious to find an ally in the rear against the Sassanid Persians (late sixth century). This prolonged struggle between Byzantium and the Sassanids which lasted, with breaks and varying fortunes, over half a century (527-591), exhausted both sides and partly explains the victories a few decades later of the Bedouin from Arabia, inspired by Islam. As for the Eastern Tu-chueh, they had difficulties with the Chinese who played on tribal rivalries and allied with the Western Tu-chueh to take the former from behind. But the Chinese suffered defeat at the hands of the Koreans (612-614) and a civil war broke out.

T'ang China

The Tu-chueh returned to the attack, taking advantage of the disorders, and threatened the capital at Chang-an. However, the emperor T'ai Tsong (627-649) succeeded in destroying the power of the eastern Tu-chueh.

For half a century, the khaghan was subject to China (630-682). Then, as with the T'ang dynasty (618-907), it was a time of offensives, it was soon the turn of the western Tu-chueh. Divisions and splits were actively encouraged (642-651). The Chinese exercised a protectorate over the Tarim and, from that base, stepped up their pressure. The western Tu-chueh collapsed in turn (657). Under the emperor T'ai-tsung, T'ang China was once again, as in the time of the Han five centuries before, mistress of High Asia as far as Turkestan.

The Orkhon inscriptions say:[5] "Because of the disorders between nobles and their subjects, because of ruse and deceit, Chinese who set younger brother against elder brother, nobles against those without rank, the people caused the disintegration of the empire that had been its own, precipitating the ruin of the khaghans who had been its khaghans..."

Everything in the steppes was fluid and provisional. Defeats signified less annihilation than flight after a reverse, and the first sign of weakening on the part of the adversary would provoke a return to the offensive. Thus, after an eclipse of thirty years, a khaghan, Elteris, nicknamed the Fortunate (Qutlu), reconstituted what is known as the second Turkish khaghanate (682-744).

According to the Chinese chronicles, the Tu-chueh revered their khaghan as a semi-divine being, obeyed his orders to the letter and were respectful of hierarchy. Before battle, the drum was sounded. Orders were communicated by a horn. To charge, they put themselves in order and attacked in arrow formation. Their heavy cavalry had armor made of metal or strips of hardened leather. The horses were caparisoned. The elite archers wore a bird of prey's feather on their helmets. In hand-to-hand fighting they used the lance or straight sword. Their infantry was transported on camel back. Half a dozen raids against China followed one after the other (685-702). The T'ang resisted, although fighting on several fronts, and, by 714, had retaken control of Zungharia while the second khaghanate went into rapid decline. The khaghan of the Tu-chueh allied with China against the Kitan nomads (also known as Khitaï) who were being very threatening. In the middle of the century (744) the khaganate collapsed under attacks by the Turkic-speaking Uighurs.

***

The second half of the seventh century and the first half of the eighth was a time of great upheavals in central Asia. On the one hand, the Arabs, who had taken Syria from the Byzantines in 636 and destroyed the Sassanid dynasty in 643, reached Bactria in 705, and Bukhara four years later, and in 712 drove out the ruler of Ferghana, who sought support from the T'ang; the first shock of Arab penetration was taken by the Western Tu-chueh. On the other hand, the Tibetans were in full expansion. By 670, they had reached the Tarim. The previous year, they had defeated the T'ang troops in eastern Turkestan and, in twenty years, they extended their empire over much of central Asia. The Tibetans sought to make an alliance with the caliphate of Baghdad against China. Five years later, the Tibetans and Chinese were fighting each other for control of Gilgit (northern Pakistan).

At this time, in the middle of the eighth century, four powers had imperial designs:

- The Arabs, whose advance guard, backed by Qarluq Turks, defeated Chinese forces at the battle on the Talas river, in Kirghizstan in 751. Shortly after, China experienced a bitter civil war (755-763), which paralyzed any prospect of a counter-attack.

- The Chinese, who were at a peak in this period with their campaign west of the Pamirs in 750 against the Tibetans, at that time more formidable adversaries than the Arabs they had met on the Talas river.

- The Tibetans, whose empire reached its peak in the second half of the century (755-797), seized control of a large area; after taking one of the Chinese capitals, Chang-an, they signed a treaty with China stipulating that they controlled eastern Turkestan, Kansu, and part of Szechuan. Their influence extended as far as Bengal, whose ruler acknowledged their suzerainty. Buddhism was declared the state religion in 779. The Tibetans tried to seize Chang-an a second time in 789, but failed.

Harun al-Rashid, Caliph of Baghdad (786-809), worried by the rising power of the Tibetans, broke off his alliance with them and renewed negotiations with China. A Chinese offensive into Turkestan was halted in 791, not by the Tibetans who had concentrated the bulk of their forces against China, but by Turkish tribes who withstood the Chinese and Uighurs. The Tibetan empire, too vast for a tiny population, collapsed (842).

- Finally, a fourth power: the Uighurs, who after destroying the second khaghanate then established one of the great empires of High Asia, which survived for a century (744-840). The Uighurs created a centralized empire with its capital at Karabalghasun. They were allies of China that China preferred to see as clients. They fought the Tibetans and came to the aid of the T'ang when the latter had to put down the major rebellion led by An Lu-shan (a Turkish-speaking mercenary) who almost brought down the dynasty (755-763). They came back a second time to lend their help against retribution (762-770). Meanwhile, while he was on a visit to China (762), the khaghan of the Uighurs converted to Manichaeism, a religion of Iranian origin founded by Mani and built on the opposition between the principles of good and evil. Manichaeism, adopted as the state religion, played a major civilizing role in the history of the Uighurs.

The inscription on the Orkhon of their capital Karabalghasun (early ninth century) comments, no doubt in a somewhat idealized way, on the conversion of the Uighurs to Manichaeism: "This country with its barbarian customs and running with blood was transformed into a country where vegetables were eaten, the country where people were encouraged to do good." In fact, the increasingly powerful Uighurs put pressure on China to obtain the most material benefits possible.

The Uighurs fought the Tibetans with varying fortunes (790-792). The Tibetans at one point even threatened the capital of Karabalghasun itself (816). With a veneer of Chinese and Sogdian (at that time Manichaean) culture, and with a script that was taken up by the Mongols and then the Manchus, the Uighurs played a major cultural role in the history of central Asia. Their decline began in about 820, with palace intrigues, rebellions, and the appearance in the north of Kirghiz power. The Kirghiz, invited by a Uighur leader in a factional dispute, penetrated the weakened empire. They administered its coup de grâce by killing the khaghan and seizing the capital (840). (The Ming would later commit the same mistake by calling on the help of the Manchus in the seventeenth century.)

It had taken the formidable power of the T'ang dynasty and the depth of China to withstand the threefold pressure from the Tu-chueh, the Arabs, and above all the Tibetans. It is true that the western regions were lost, but the empire had resisted and survived all its adversaries.

One nomad wave was no sooner exhausted than another pushed it aside or replaced it. The Kirghiz controlled Upper Mongolia but were dislodged by proto-Mongols, the Khitans or Khitaï. Already, at the very end of the seventh century, a Khitan leader, from the forests of Manchuria, had declared himself khaghan and challenged the Chinese. The Khitans originally came from the northern province of Jehol and are mentioned by that name on the Orkhon inscriptions. Under the T'ang (618-906), they were successively, in light of changing relations of force, allies and adversaries of China.

To cut the new khaghan down to size, the Chinese launched a campaign, but to no effect. There had to be negotiations. The Khitan ruler received a Chinese princess in marriage for the first time. But before long, there was a new Khitan incursion followed by a Chinese counter-attack. The results were not decisive and in 745 there was a return to treaty-making and marriage alliances.

The Khitans at first declared themselves vassals of the Uighurs, but in 842 acknowledged Chinese suzerainty. A-pao-chi (872-926) succeeded in uniting the Khitan tribes. Until then, the eight tribes composing the Khitan people retained their prerogatives and the leader was chosen among them every three years.

For his part, A-pao-chi took the title of emperor and founded the Liao dynasty (907-1125). The weakening of Chinese power once again favored the nomads. By 947 the Khitan rulers had made themselves masters of most of northern China. The political fragmentation of China accelerated and lasted all through the Sung dynasty (960-1234). For three or four centuries the Ordos bend ceased to be under Chinese control.

By 960, the Khitans were already confronting the Sung and soon extracted a treaty from them (1005). This laid down that the Sung would pay the Liao state of the Khitans a tribute of 100,000 ounces of silver and 200,000 bolts of silk. A generation later, the power of the Sung had further diminished and they had to concede more: 200,000 ounces of silver and 300,000 bolts of silk. Meanwhile, the Khitans had adopted Buddhism and were becoming sinicized.

In a process so predictable because so repetitive, these nomad creators of a state based on the Chinese model soon had to deal with pressure from newcomers. The Jurchens, subjects of the Khitans, were growing stronger and beginning to assert themselves and then challenged their masters. They were soon in open conflict. Like the Khitans, the Jurchens were originally from the forests of Manchuria. They had that furious drive that was characteristic of the nomads of the time when they launched their onslaughts. It had been the same with the Khitans in their day, before they settled in towns and profited from the surplus extracted from the peasants and the initial aggressiveness was toned down with the adoption of Buddhism, as was the case with the Wei. The war between the Jurchens and the Khitans ended in an initial defeat for the latter (1114). Seven years later, the Jurchens took the capital of the state of Liao. The following year, with the Sung only too happy to find an ally in their enemy's rear, the Jurchens crushed the Khitans (1125). The Jurchens became the masters of northern China and founded a dynasty (Chin, 1115-1234). Taking advantage of the weakening of China following the T'ang dynasty, the Khitans and the Jurchens appear as precursors of the Mongols whose onslaught would roll over northern China a century later and conquer the whole of the Middle Kingdom for the first time.

The Khitans, defeated by the Jurchens, did not disappear from history like so many peoples absorbed or scattered who have left hardly a trace. A large body of Khitans left northern China in 1124 and made towards the Tarim basin. After defeating the Karakanid state and beating the Seljukids, these Khitans created an empire, called Qara Khitaï (or Western Liao for the Chinese) whose capital was Balasaghun. Their ruler boasted the title of *gür khan* (universal khan) and the empire stretched from the northern border of China to the Aral Sea.

The Buddhist *gür khan*'s victory over the Seljukids, that is over Islam, became known in Europe and was the origin of the legend of "Prester John," the providential ally who it was hoped would come to the aid of the Crusaders by taking the Muslims from the rear. The Qara Khitaï empire lasted until it was divided among the Naimans, allies of Genghis Khan, and the ruler of the state of Khorezm in 1211. Some of the Khitans stayed in China under Jurchen rule. They revolted several times (1161, 1169, 1177). When the Mongols arrived in China in 1211, many Khitans collaborated with them.

Like all nomad groups, the Jurchens were mounted archers, organized on the decimal system. The first Jurchen emperor, the founder of the Chin dynasty (1115), inherited the Liao empire created by the Khitans; the second extended his domain to embrace much of northern China with his capital at K'ai-feng (1128). It is estimated that by the beginning of the thirteenth century, the Chin state had some forty million inhabitants, a figure that no state outside China came even near at the time, and much higher than the figure for the Liao state. Before long a peace treaty, embellished as usual with tribute, was signed with Sung China (1142), which temporarily stabilized the situation. An attempt by the Jurchens to penetrate into Sung territory was a total failure (1161). But the rise of the Mongols soon transformed the Chin state into a buffer state between the Sung and the Mongols. The sinicization of the Jurchens seems to have been even more rapid and more complete than that of the Khitans. Chin resistance to the Mongol advance went on for over two decades before a combined attack by the Mongols and the Sung in 1233-1234 put an end to their dynasty. The Jurchens fell back on Manchuria where they maintained their independence.

In the fifteenth and sixteenth centuries the Jurchens once again became a power. Their ruler took the title of representative of the "Later Chin" in 1616, thus laying claim to continuity with the dynasty that reigned over northern China in the twelfth and thirteenth centuries. More importantly, these Jurchens were the ancestors of the Manchus who seized the whole of China in 1644.

Meanwhile, at the beginning of the thirteenth century, the Mongols burst onto the world stage.

The Indo-Iranian Front

Whoever controls the world of Iran is already at the gates of India. The world of Iran, across Afghanistan, through which every invader of northern India had to pass, lay on the very threshold of the steppes of central Asia and, were it not for the barrier of the Oxus, might be regarded as simply an extension of them. Yet history as well as geography has endorsed this break. Iran was founded on an ancient and brilliant urban civilization and a refined system of irrigation.

All the nomads of High Asia at one time or another were pressing on the borders of Iran and often penetrated there, both before and after its Islamization in the seventh century. *Responding to pressure*

*from the nomads in the north was one of the constant features of
Iran's external policy.*

In a first phase, one on which archaeology provides much information, Iran suffered incursions by the Scythians, the Sarmatians,
and those whom the Chinese chronicles call the Yüeh-chih (140-
130 B.C.). At the beginning of the Christian era, these latter formed a
vast empire, known as the Kushan empire, which stretched from the
Aral Sea to the Punjab. This empire reached its apogee when, having converted to Buddhism, they had a ruler named Kanishka (first
century A.D.).

Better known to people in the West was the empire founded by
the Parthians (Arcasids, c.250 B.C.-A.D. 226) whose manner of fighting, famous since the disaster inflicted on the Roman legions at
Carrhae in 53 B.C., derived directly from nomad tactics.

While the Black Huns who had pillaged Asia Minor and Europe
as far as Gaul and Italy ceased to be a source of anxiety in the second half of the fifth century, the Hephthalite (White) Huns were ex-
panding all the time. They originally came from the steppes, between Lake Balkash and the Sea of Azov, and they pillaged Khorasan
and occupied Merv and Herat. Sassanid Iran (226-642) resisted. The
Hephthalites then turned against Kabul and reached Gandhara and
then Kandahar and emerged into the Punjab (c.470). Here they came
up against the Gupta empire (c.320-c.544). Two attempts at invasion were repulsed. Meanwhile, the Hephthalites won a victory over
the Sassanids and put the Iranian king to death (484). But dynastic
divisions and disputes weakened the Gupta empire which collapsed
under the attacks of the ruler of the Hephthalite Huns, Miharakula
(502-530). The nomad push out of High Asia in the fifth century
overran the whole of the Eurasian landmass.

In the sixth century, Sassanid Iran had to face pressure from the
Tu-chueh, who were allies of Byzantium between 584 and 594. Long
before the coming of Islam, Iran was one of those privileged regions
where, through urban centers where trade was carried on, nomads
began to learn about the ways of sedentary life. Worn out by a long
struggle with Byzantium, the Sassanids collapsed in a few years before the triumphal onslaught of the Arabs. The Arabs overran the
Iranian empire between 636 and 642. The battle of Qasidiya (636,
in Iraq) and the battle of Nehavend (642, in Iran) marked the last
five years of a glorious empire whose last ruler disappeared in
643.

After a brief halt, the Arab advance resumed even more impetuously and at the beginning of the eighth century penetrated central Asia, reaching the farthest point of western central Asia in 751. In that year, Arab troops, backed up by Qarluq Turks clashed with the Chinese troops of the T'ang. These latter were defeated and the Chinese withdrawal was under way. The *bilad al islam* (land of Islam) grew larger, although the peoples only became Islamized much later.

In the middle of the eighth century, the Abbassid dynasty chose Baghdad as its capital, and Persian cultural influence was considerable. Under the authority of the Caliph, the Samanid dynasty installed in western Iran became the shield of Islam against the Turkish and infidel nomads. As emirs of the Caliph they made themselves masters of Transoxiana for over a century (875-999). They waged a victorious campaign against the Qarluq Turks in 893, but had to face a counter-attack not long after (903).

Like the Abbassids, the Samanids employed *ghulams* (slaves taken in raids in central Asia and trained to become soldiers and sometimes officials). This system of recruitment preceded that of the janissaries instituted three centuries later. As the tenth century advanced, the proportion of ghulams of Turkish origin became higher and higher and they began more and more to assert their independence. Thus, in the second half of the tenth century, a ghulam named Alp Tegin, who commanded the army of Khorasan while acknowledging that he was a vassal of the Samanids, effectively ruled autonomously at Ghazni (969).

Not long after, one of his successors, Mahmud of Ghazni, increased his power while remaining nominally under the suzerainty of the Samanids. These latter, ever more hard pressed by the Karakanids, a Muslim dynasty that was threatening Bukhara (992), asked the Ghaznavids to intervene. They restored order and were rewarded: Mahmud officially became governor of Khorasan.

The Samanids soon disappeared, a people who had made its contribution both to the Islamization of central Asia—at the same time disseminating Persian culture—and, as Sunnis, to the fight against the Shiite Buyids.

***

At the beginning of the tenth century, the steppes of High Asia saw large population movements. The shock waves of these migrations reached the western part of High Asia in the second quarter of the eleventh century. Those who were to become known as the Seljukids were at the end of the chain when they advanced on Khorasan. In 1040, near Merv, the Seljukids defeated the Ghaznavids who fell back and went and occupied the Punjab. Eastern Iran fell into the hands of the Seljukids. As for the western part of Iran, it was ruled by the Buyids (932-1055), who were Persian by culture and Shiites. The Seljukids helped the Caliph to get rid of the Buyids (1055) and, at once, Toghrul Bey, the leader of the Seljukids, became even more important after he had crushed a revolt fomented by one of his relatives, who had converted to Shiism and proclaimed the removal of the Caliph.

In 1060, Toghrul Bey, restorer of the Caliph and guardian of Muslim orthodoxy, became the founder of an Iranized Turkic sultanate, which took over the role hitherto played by the Samanids.

Toghrul's nephew, Alp Arslan, succeeded him (1063-1072). He first had to eliminate a cousin who wanted power (among the nomads, dynastic succession was open to uncles, nephews, brothers, and even cousins; the principle of primogeniture was unknown). Then he made himself master of the whole of Iran and had the good sense to take on the great Persian Nizam al-Mulk (1018-1092) as minister. The Seljukids modeled themselves closely on the Samanids.

In 1071, Alp Arslan won the victory of Manzikert[6] and took the Byzantine emperor Romanus Diogenes prisoner, later releasing him. But as the tenth century came to an end Asia Minor was above all raiding territory.

Alp Arslan died in 1072. The reign of his successor, Malik Shah (1072-1092), marked the zenith of the Seljukid empire of Iran. The Seljukids defeated the Karakanids and extended their empire northward: Samarqand and Bukhara were taken. The khaghan of the Karakanids submitted after a campaign that took the Seljukids as far as Talas. But, the situation deteriorated rapidly. Kara-Khitaï inflicted a heavy defeat on the Seljukids in 1141.

On the eve of the Mongol invasion, the situation in the Iranian area in its widest sense was as follows:

A recently formed empire that lacked cohesion, called Khorezm, was stretching from central Asia to the borders of India.

Between the end of the fifth and the eleventh century, for half a millennium, India, protected by its relative geographical marginality, largely escaped invasion. Part of Sind was occupied by the Muslims in the eighth century while, at the end of the same century, a Muslim attack on the Deccan was driven back.

The Muslim incursions resumed with Mahmud of Ghazni. He launched ten whose aim was pillage, not occupation. Mahmud devastated the imperial city of Kannawj and the holy city of Mathura. After his death, India enjoyed a respite of sixty years—until 1192 when Mohammed Gur defeated the forces of the last Hindu king of Delhi. A sultanate was soon established, in 1206, and northern India remained under the rule of sultans of Turkic origin until its conquest by Babur, the founder of the Mughal dynasty, in 1526. Babur was a descendant of the Timurids, and had been driven out of Samarqand by the Uzbeks; he withdrew to Kabul and embarked on the conquest of India from Afghanistan. His reign was short (1526-1530). But the dynasty that he founded, which came to dominate almost the whole of India, lasted essentially until the British took control.

The Byzantine Front

The Byzantine empire, a Christian state whose capital was founded in 330, survived for a thousand years after the fall of Rome in 476, until 1453 when the city was taken by the Ottomans. It was the heir of Rome administratively and juristically, but Greek soon replaced Latin linguistically and culturally. Thus, it can be said that it was the heir of Rome politically, of Greece culturally, and of Christianity spiritually.

After successfully containing the Goths in the fifth century, the empire enjoyed a short but remarkable period of expansion. Half a century after the fall of Rome, the Roman emperor Justinian (527-565), who was responsible for a famous code, undertook a reconquest that was initially very successful. Thanks to two outstanding generals, Belisarius and Narses, the Byzantines briefly regained control of north Africa (533), Italy (535-554), and southern Spain (552).

But before long, with bubonic plague ravaging their troops, the Byzantines had to face three threats: the Slavs in the Balkans, the Sassanids in Iran, and the Lombards in Italy. The effort to restore the empire and the rising number of threats precipitated a serious financial and social crisis of which the Sassanids took advantage to attack the empire with their Avar and Slav allies. The Byzantines were in grave danger, yet managed to resist the Avar nomads who were harassing them along the Danube frontier from where they launched deep incursions. The emperor Maurice (582-602) successfully contained the Avars and repulsed the Sassanids.

We know about the Avars from a series of accounts and chronicles, in Greek, Syriac, Armenian, Coptic, and other languages. While, in the middle of the sixth century, the Tu-chueh founded an empire embracing the whole of High Asia, after overcoming the Juan-juan and the Hephthalite Huns, those called Avars fled westward. Some of them fought on the side of the emperor Justinian (c. 562) when he was in the midst of his territorial reconquests. The main body of the Avars fought unsuccessfully with the Franks and then succeeded in occupying Pannonia (Hungary) (568). In 571, a treaty was signed with the Byzantine empire, which dominated all the land south of the Danube. Like all treaties signed between nomads and sedentary peoples, it was fragile and was soon broken. The Byzantines were soon defeated and had to negotiate another treaty (578) by which they agreed, in exchange for an alliance with the Avars, to pay them eighty million pieces of gold each year. There are many Byzantine sources (John of Ephesus, Menander Protector and above all Theophylact Simocattes), but no one informs us better about the military aspect than the emperor Maurice (582-602) in the work attributed to him the *Strategikon*:

> Dealing with the Scythians, That is, Avars, Turks, and Others Whose Way of Life Resembles That of the Hunnish Peoples
>
> The Scythian nations are one, so to speak, in their mode of life and in their organization, which is primitive and includes many peoples. Of these peoples, only the Turks and the Avars concern themselves with military organization, and this makes them stronger than the other Scythian nations when it comes to pitched battles. The nation of the Turks is very numerous and independent. They are not versatile or skilled in most human endeavors, nor have they trained themselves for anything except to conduct themselves bravely against their enemies. The Avars, for their part, are scoundrels, devious, and very experienced in military matters.
>
> These nations have a monarchical form of government, and their rulers subject them to cruel punishments for their mistakes. Governed not by love but by fear, they steadfastly bear labors and hardships. They endure heat and cold, and the want of many necessities, since they are nomadic peoples. They are very superstitious, treacherous, foul, faithless, possessed by an insatiate desire for riches. They scorn their oath, do not observe agreements, and are not satisfied by gifts. Even before they accept the gift, they are making plans for treachery and betrayal of their agreements. They are clever at estimating suitable opportunities to do this and taking prompt advantage of them. They prefer to prevail over their enemies not so much by force as by deceit, surprise attacks, and cutting off supplies.
>
> They are armed with mail, swords, bows, and lances. In combat most of them attack doubly armed; lances slung over their shoulders and holding bows in their hands, they

make use of both as need requires. Not only do they wear armor themselves, but in addition the horses of their illustrious men are covered in front with iron or felt. They give special attention to training in archery on horseback.

A vast herd of male and female horses follow them, both to provide nourishment and to give the impression of a huge army. They do not encamp within entrenchments, as do the Persians and the Romans, but until the day of battle, spread about according to tribes and clans, they continuously graze their horses both summer and winter. Then they take the horses they think necessary, hobbling them next to their tents, and guard them until it is time to form their battle line, which they begin to do under cover of night. They station their sentries at some distance, keeping them in contact with one another, so that it is not easy to catch them by a surprise attack.

In combat they do not, as do the Romans and Persians, form their battle line in three parts, but in several units of irregular size, all joined closely together to give the appearance of one long battle line. Separate from their main formation, they have an additional force which they can send out to ambush a careless adversary or hold in reserve to aid a hard-pressed section...

They prefer battles fought at long range, ambushes, encircling their adversaries, simulated retreats and sudden returns, and wedge-shaped formations, that is, in scattered groups. When they make their enemies take to flight, they put everything else aside, and are not content, as the Persians, the Romans, and other peoples, with pursuing them a reasonable distance and plundering their goods, but they do not let up at all until they have achieved the complete destruction of their enemies."[7]

The Avars were not the Byzantines' first nomad adversaries. As the *Strategikon* points out, they had experienced the Turks. As early as the fifth century, the Byzantines had sought an alliance with the Turks of central Asia against the Sassanids. During the second half of the sixth century (c. 576), the Turks turned against the Byzantines in the Crimea—which was a serious blow to the empire's trade. But Byzantium contained the Turks, as it later contained many other adversaries, until their lack of unity brought them to blows with one another, as so often happens with tribal peoples.

Several times, the Avars got near Constantinople. In 582, they laid siege to the capital. Slav troops and Gepids had joined the khaghan of the Avars. The Sassanids hastened to join but were unable to cross the arm of the sea that separates Asia from Europe, which had been blocked by the Byzantine fleet. Indeed, it was the fleet, which, after ten fruitless days of siege and assaults, was decisive. The ships of the "Rus" (as the Slavs of Russia were then known) were destroyed by Greek fire in the Golden Horn. The Avars, impotent before the walls of Constantinople, withdrew.

But the Avars themselves were being harassed by the Oghuz Turks who had reached the Chersonesus (Crimea) by 585 and were only just holding them off. The following year, the Avars laid siege to Thessalonika. From now on the imperial tribute paid by Constantinople to have peace on this front and be able to devote its attention to the chief adversary, the Sassanids, amounted to one hundred thousand pieces of gold. That did not prevent the Byzantines from taking the offensive on a number of occasions to reduce the pressure from the Avars. In 599-600, the Byzantine general Priscus crossed the Danube and struck the Avars on their territory; the following year (601), he defeated the Avars. Nevertheless, no victory against the nomads was decisive, as they simply withdrew after a setback and came back once their strength had been rebuilt.

No state, except China, experienced such a variety of adversaries over a period of a thousand years and more or succeeded almost unbrokenly in surviving and adapting to the enemy's mode of combat while at the same time knowing how to use whatever allies might be available in order to hold back the principal adversary of the moment. Like the Chinese, the Byzantines were past masters in the art of using Barbarians against Barbarians.

In 619, the Avars almost captured the Byzantine emperor Heraclius (610-641). He had to pay an annual tribute of two hundred thousand pieces of gold and hand his son over as hostage to ensure a truce while he waged all-out war against the Sassanids.

At the request of Heraclius, ever in quest of allies in his enemies' rear, the Khazars, who had recently founded a powerful state, agreed to ally with the Byzantines against the Sassanids (622-627). Heraclius succeeded in turning round a situation that was indeed desperate. Thanks to a combined naval and land operation, the Sassanid forces were taken from the rear. The Byzantines were finally victorious and restored the empire to its original borders. Shortly after, the khaghanate of the Western Turks, which had been the Bzyantines' ally against the Sassanids, collapsed (630).

Hardly had Byzantine power been restored than the emperor had to deal with an even more serious threat. Carried along by the religious zeal born of the preaching of Mahomet (died 632), and seeking to spread the message of the Prophet, the Arabs took advantage of the exhaustion of the Sassanids and the Byzantines after several decades of conflict. In 636, they defeated the Byzantine army at Yarmuk; a few months later, at Qadisiya, they beat the Sassanid forces and then put an end to the Sassanid empire at the battle of Nehavend (642). In the same year, they invaded Egypt. Alexandria alone held out until 647. Generally, in Syria as in Egypt, the Christian populations, who had not accepted the Byzantine orthodoxy laid down by the Council of Chalcedon (451), were oppressed and heavily taxed by the Byzantines and rather welcomed the new conquerors who showed more tolerance. On the death of Heraclius (641), the Byzantine empire, which had once ruled half the Mediterranean world, was reduced to Asia Minor, the coastal fringe of the Balkans, Sicily, and a small part of north Africa.

The decades that followed could easily have been the Byzantine empire's last years. The Arab threat hung over Asia Minor, and Arab troops often came through the Cilician gates to ravage Anatolia. Furthermore, these nomads who, forty years before, knew nothing about communications except the camel, built a fleet and, in 673-678, threatened Constantinople from the sea.

While the Avars and the Arabs continued to be a threatening presence, the appearance of the Bulgars, who had come from central Asia at the beginning of the sixth century, soon represented a new threat. The first waves of Bulgars who clashed with the Avars were driven back by these latter and attempted to move into Bavaria where they were massacred by the troops of Dagobert, king of the Franks. But other waves of Bulgars, in larger numbers, poured in and settled in what was to become Bulgaria (c. 680) where they gradually became Slavized. They created a kingdom there (681) while another branch of the Bulgars settled along the Volga.

With periods of remission even after their conversion to Christianity (864), the Bulgar threat continued to be one of the major preoccupations of the Byzantine empire from the end of the seventh century to the beginning of the eleventh.

Yet, at the end of the seventh century and the beginning of the eighth, the Arab danger outranked all others since the war with the Sassanids. Carthage had fallen in 697, north Africa was being overrun. And in 717-718, the Arab fleet again laid siege to Constantinople. Once again, thanks to Greek fire, the siege was lifted. The halt to Muslim penetration imposed by the Byzantine empire was of an altogether greater significance than Charles Martel's victory over an Arab detachment at Poitiers in 732.

The empire was able to triumph thanks to the efforts of two great military emperors (Leo III the Isaurian, 717-741, and Constantine V,

741-775), and the Slav, Avar, Arab, and Bulgar threats were halted. But the empire that emerged from these tremendous challenges was a much diminished one. At least half the territories that had been Byzantine were lost, most of them permanently. In the eighth century, apart from a brief interval under the Macedonian dynasty, Byzantine imperial strategy was fundamentally defensive. Even this recovery was short-lived. While Charlemagne, crowned emperor in 800 in the West, put down the Avars, the Byzantine empire was once again assailed by the Bulgars and the Arabs.

All through this period, the alliance with the Khazars held good. The son of the emperor Constantine V was born of a Khazar princess and when he reigned (775-780), he was nicknamed "the Khazar." In the middle of the ninth century, a Khazar khaghan embraced Judaism, according to the Arab historian al-Masudi, but Judaism was not made the state religion. Islam was present also, and converts included some high-ranking dignitaries. In fact, the Khazars were only identified with Judaism in Egypt and Spain. In the mid-ninth century the area they dominated stretched from the Volga delta to the northern Caucasus and from the Don to the borders of the Abbassid caliphate and the Byzantine empire.

The Khazars fought the Rus who, after a vain attempt to take Constantinople in 860, ravaged part of their possessions and were only contained with great difficulty. Soon (861) a new wave of nomads appeared who would fight the Byzantine empire, the Khazars, and Kievan Russia: the Pechenegs. These nomads, who were, in turn, being pressed upon by the Oghuz Turks and by a shock wave that was driving the Hungarians westward, constituted a threat for the Byzantine empire for over a century and a half. They crossed the Danube and threatened the Balkans where they made frequent incursions.

The great Byzantine dynasty known as the Macedonian dynasty (867-1057) began with the Armenian emperor Basil I who, in twenty years, taking advantage of the break-up of the Arab caliphate into rival kingdoms, succeeded in reconquering most of Syria and part of Mesopotamia. This dynasty marked the zenith of the medieval glory of the Byzantine empire. It was during the reign of the "Macedonians" that the conversion to Christianity of the Bulgars (864) and the Russians (988) occurred. But the security of the empire was never truly re-established. There were too many adversaries, sedentary peoples, newly settled nomads or new nomadic waves who renewed their assaults: Arabs, Bulgars, Russians, Pechenegs.

The Russians landed on the coast of Thrace in 941 and ravaged it before they were driven out. In alliance with the Pecheneg nomads, they launched a new offensive in 944 which produced more results since they succeeded in obtaining a tribute from the Byzantine empire in exchange for a treaty.

Under an outstanding general, John Tzimisces (969-976), half of Bulgaria was conquered, a Russian invasion was halted, and an offensive took Byzantine troops almost to Jerusalem. Constantinople used the Pechenegs against the ruler of Kiev (972). But they were allies only when it suited them and they ravaged the empire on many occasions. Basil II, known as Bulgaroctonus ("slayer of the Bulgars," 996-1025), finally crushed the Bulgars. On his death the decline of Constantinople began, first barely noticeably then more rapidly during the twelfth century, so that after the sack of Constantinople by the Crusaders in 1204, it entered a slow agony.

The Byzantine Defensive Model

In order to be able to hold out for a thousand years against a host of sedentary or nomad adversaries, the Byzantine empire had to combine a diplomacy based on a sharp political sense with strategic thinking that produced a series of theoretical treatises between the seventh and eleventh centuries, and an unrivaled capacity to adapt.

After the failure of the reconquest waged by Justinian in the sixth century, the emperors Tiberius and Maurice reorganized the army and put it firmly under the command of the emperor and not of the generals who recruited mercenaries. Better still, Maurice wanted territorial forces built on the mobilization of free men. It was the army formed by Tiberius and Maurice that the emperor Hercalius led to victory against the Sassanids of Iran (seventh century). The heavy cavalry, made up of *cataphracts*, was one of its key features.

In the following century, while the Near East and Egypt were lost, the Isaurians perfected the system of *themai*, each province having a standing force of soldiers/peasants designed to receive the first shock of any possible attack. The thematic army was an army in the image of an empire that, apart from Justinian and the so-called Macedonian dynasty (especially in the ninth-tenth centuries), was mainly on the defensive. In that respect, the parallel with China is indeed striking. Apart from the Han and the T'ang, and, briefly at the beginning of the Ming dynasty, China was, especially in the north, a defensive empire.

In addition to the provincial themes, the empire set up special forces with the responsibility of guarding the mountain passes. These were the *akritai*. They were frontier troops par excellence and were celebrated in the Byzantine epic *Digenis Akritas*. The Byzantine army at its peak had some one hundred and twenty thousand men, seventy thousand of whom were stationed in the east, and the rest on the Danube and in the center. On several occasions, the navy proved to be decisive, and it played a key role right up to the beginning of the eleventh century. It was divided into two themes: one for the Aegean and one for the coast of Asia Minor. Its ships, *dromons*, dominated the Mediterranean.

With regard to relations with the peoples of the steppe, it was the general of the Chersonesus (Crimea) who organized missions and contacts and collected information. Embassies sent to the Khazar allies, alliances of circumstance with the Pechenegs against the Bulgars, or with the Magyars (Hungarians) against the Pechenegs, were above all negotiated from the Chersonesus.

In the year following the death of Basil II (1026), the Pechenegs were driven back on the Danube. But their pressure grew relentlessly: they were themselves being pressed by the Oghuz Turks (ancestors of the Turkmens) and they invaded the empire en masse (1051). The Pechenegs penetrated into Thrace and advanced to the gates of Constantinople. Once again, the walls and the city's geographical location were more than the assailants could overcome. In the mid-eleventh century, the major upheavals in central Asia meant that the Oghuz themselves were being pressed upon by a wave of new nomad conquerors, the Kipchaks, also Turkic-speakers. As the Oghuz were being defeated by a coalition of the Pechenegs and the Bulgars (c. 1055), the Normans were driving the Byzantines out of southern Italy and Sicily. The great schism between the Eastern Church and the Western Church was consummated in 1054. Some of the Oghuz Turks went over to the service of Byzantium on the Danube frontier, while others launched a series of raids against the empire in Thrace (1064-1065).

But a new danger was appearing in the east: the Seljukids who, under the leadership of Alp Arslan, defeated the Byzantine army at Manzikert in Armenia and took the emperor prisoner. A contingent of mercenaries, Pecheneg horsemen, who went over to the Seljukids, perhaps helped decide the day. Manzikert opened Asia Minor to Turkish penetration. But nothing was yet settled. There were endless tribal disputes among the Turks and perhaps the last of the truly great Byzantine emperors was Alexius Comnenus (1081-1118), who played Suleiman ibn Kutulmush, an ally of the Byzantines, against his cousin Alp Arslan at Nicaea.

In 1088-1089, the Pechenegs penetrated as far as Adrianople. The emperor Alexius Comnenus negotiated and bought peace at a time when the principal danger lay now in the east. Even so, he had to fight on every front at once: the Normans in the western Mediterranean, the Pechenegs in the north, the Turks in the east.

The arrival of the Crusaders (1096-1099) allowed Alexius Comnenus to retake Nicaea, which was in the hands of the Turks, but his reign was simply one last moment of grandeur. The Byzantine currency, which, for six centuries, had been a sort of gold standard in Mediterranean trade, lost its value. Venice already coveted the place so long occupied by Constantinople. In 1090, while the Seljukids were threatening Nicomedia and the Pecheneg threat was as great as ever, Alexius Comnenus turned to the Kipchaks, who had come from central Asia and were now pushing up against the empire on the steppes to the north. Byzantine and Kipchak forces crushed the Pechenegs (1091). It was a decisive blow. Thirty years later, the Pechenegs tried one last time, with reduced means, to penetrate into Bulgaria. They were finally crushed (1122) and some of them became *foederati* along the Danube. Meanwhile, the Seljukids of Iran had been swept aside by the Qara Khitaï (Buddhists) in 1092.

The First Crusade altered the regional military situation. The Turkish drive westward was halted. The Turks were defeated at Dorylaeum (1096); and before long Antioch, Edessa, and Jerusalem were being taken by the Latin Crusaders. The Turkish drive into Europe only really resumed in the fourteenth century, two hundred and fifty years later. Conversely, the Turkish presence in Asia Minor increased during the second half of the twelfth century; this was the consequence of the Mongol conquests that precipitated the flight of large numbers of Turkomans who formed small, fervently conquering Muslim principalities in Anatolia on the frontiers. The Seljukid Kilij Arslan II conquered part of central Anatolia, which led other Turkish principalities (the *Danishmendids*) to appeal to the Byzantine emperor for help, and he, worried by the rising power of Kilij Arslan, resolved to confront him, only to be crushingly defeated at Myriakephalon (1176). It was a defeat as clear-cut as the one at Manzikert and much more serious since it showed that even after a century the empire had been unable to recreate a high-quality army.

Byzantine decline, already palpable economically, became obvious in matters military after Myriakephalon. It was a disaster that, this time, showed that the Turks were solidly implanted in Anatolia. The Byzantine army was no more than a shadow of what it had been. Worse, in 1204, Constantinople, the commercial rival of Venice, was sacked by the Crusaders. After more than half a century of exile at Nicaea, the Byzantine emperors returned to power in 1261. But the city was depopulated and ruined. In the meanwhile, the Seljukids of the sultanate of Rum, with its capital at Konya, had been crushed by the Mongols in 1243 near Erzinjan. The only thing that was settled, apparently, was the decline of Byzantium.

The great Mongol drive in Asia brought a band of fleeing Turks to the neighborhood of the capital; this was the embryo of what, after Osman (1299-1326), would become the Ottoman empire. The Byzantine empire's decision to bring in mercenaries belonging to the Catalan Grand Company in 1302 to defend it, proved a serious error. Constantinople was blockaded for two years (1305-1307), while Macedonia was pillaged.

The Ottomans began to advance into the Balkans in the mid-fourteenth century. They took Adrianople in 1357 and made it their capital. They fought the Bulgars and then made themselves masters of Serbia, at the time the most powerful of the Balkan kingdoms (Kosovo, 1389), and reached the Danube. For the Byzantine empire that for at least two centuries had been being nibbled away at in Asia Minor, the capture of the Balkans by the Ottomans signified demographic strangulation.

Shortly after, a coalition of Western knights was defeated at Nicopolis (1398). By now, nothing, apart from the kingdom of Hungary, seemed in a position to stand up to the organization of the Ottoman army and its elite infantry corps, the janissaries. The Byzantine empire, protected by walls that could only be destroyed by appropriate artillery, was now no more than a territorially derisory left-over: the Peloponnese, Mistra, and Thessalonika.

Constantinople was besieged by the Ottomans for the first time in 1397 and the city was only temporarily reprieved thanks to Timur (Tamerlane) who overwhelmed the Ottoman sultan Bayazid at the battle of Ankara (1402). The Byzantines lacked the necessary resources in men and money to exploit this unexpected defeat of their most pugnacious adversary. Yet the empire's prestige was such that Mahomet I (1403-1421) allied with Byzantium to reconquer the emirates of Anatolia. Murad II (1421-1451) vainly laid siege to Constantinople, failed before Belgrade, was unable to overcome the Hungarian John Hunyadi, and signed a compromise peace at Szegedin. Yet, that same year (1444), a second coalition of Western forces was heavily defeated at Varna, in Bulgaria. The fate of Constantinople was sealed when the Ottomans got appropriate artillery. After an existence lasting eleven centuries and a siege that lasted seven weeks, on 29 May 1453, the emperor was killed fighting and the city was taken by the Ottomans.

Over and beyond the financial or commercial decline, one of the essential causes of the gradual decline of the Byzantine empire was *demographic* and had to with the fact that once the Ottomans had occupied the Balkans, from the second half of the fourteenth century, they imposed an ever tighter grip on it.

Unlike China, which the size of its population enabled it always to absorb its conquerors, the Byzantine empire had only a small population and, faced with the rise of the Ottomans, could not but be overwhelmed in the end.

The Russian Front

Russian history begins with the foundation by the Varangians—a Swedish branch of the sea-borne nomads, the Vikings—of Kievan Russia (ninth century). The Varangians went up the rivers and as far as Constantinople and Baghdad, for among other reasons to sell there the slaves that they had captured on the way.

The fertile lands of Kievan Russia were also the last stretch of the Asiatic steppe. Beyond Ukraine, the Eurasian steppe extended towards Wallachia and Thrace as far as Hungary. Following the Huns and the Avars, a succession of nomad peoples ravaged southern Russia and Ukraine—in the geographical sense: Hungarians, Pechenegs, Oghuz Turks, Kipchaks (Polovtsis). By the beginning of the eleventh century, the first lines of fortifications against the nomads of the steppe were built. In the middle of the same century, the Pechenegs threatened Kiev.

The Pechenegs came from central Asia from where they were driven out by a combination of Oghuz Turks and Khazars (869). Their forced migration pushed the Hungarians westward (end of the ninth century). Byzantium, at one point threatened, drove these latter back towards Pannonia (Hungary). The Pechenegs remained masters of the steppe between the Don and the Donetz. From the time they first arrived there they clashed with the Rus, in the first third of the tenth century.

They were initially in conflict with Prince Igor of Kiev and destroyed the Russian forts that were advancing southward, and then took what is now Moldova.

At the time, the Russian frontier was marked by *gorods* (fortified places) or *tshastokols* (palisades of tree trunks) whose advance southward was intended bit by bit to secure land suitable for farming.

The Russian princes and nomad tribes fought bitterly for control of the black lands of Ukraine and present-day Moldova which could feed vast flocks for one side or produce cereals for the other.

The Russian princes also wanted to secure control of the rivers that emptied into the Black Sea, the Don and the Dniepr, which were trading routes to Constantinople. As fast as the Russian princes built forts southward, the Pechenegs destroyed them and, each year, ravaged and raided the territories to the north. That, however, did not prevent the Pechenegs from being allies of the princes of Kiev against Byzantium (944) when it suited them.

Conversely, when Sviatoslav, prince of Kiev, defeated the Bulgars opposed to Byzantium (968), these latter allied with Kiev to weaken the Pechenegs. Sviatoslav then allied with the Hungarians and attacked the Byzantine empire. But John Tzimisces, the outstanding Byzantine emperor and general, defeated him (971) and Sviatoslav had to accept a peace whose terms were dictated to him. As he retreated, the Pechenegs captured him, not far from the mouths of the Dniepr, and, according to tradition, his skull was used as a drinking bowl by his victor, the nomad ruler (972).

During the reign of his successor, Vladimir, Russia embraced Christianity, following its ruler (989). Byzantium served as both a religious and a state model. The Pechenegs were still occupying both banks of the lower Dniepr and launching their annual incursions. The ruler who succeeded Vladimir, Yaroslav the Wise (1019-1054), succeeded in inflicting a heavy defeat on the Pechenegs in 1036, and they ceased to be a threat to Russia. An alliance between Russia and newcomers from the eastern steppe, the Kipchaks (called Polovtsis by the Russians), delivered them the coup de grâce (1091).

The Oghuz Turks—who in the eighth century were occupying the steppe in the region from the Syr-Daria to the Aral Sea and who had allied with the Russians in the tenth century against the Khazars (965) and then against the Bulgars (985)—reappeared in the eleventh century and threatened Russia just as the Pecheneg threat had been removed. In 1055, says the Russian chronicle "Vsevolod, brother of Iziaslav, who had just come to the throne of Kiev, marched on the *Torki*, in winter, and, defeated them, near Voïn." The Oghuz Turks were eliminated from the region by about 1070. But the Russians were never able to occupy beyond some two and fifty kilometers south of Kiev, at least before the seventeenth century.

During this time, in the eleventh and especially the twelfth century, the Russian migration movement began to turn ever more markedly northward so as to get into the forest areas, away from nomad incursions. Suzdal was founded in the tenth century, Riazan in the eleventh. In the following century, Vladimir, Moscow, Tver, and Tula became important centres. But the Russians were worried by the rise of Kipchak power and princes Vladimir Monomakh and Sviatopolk II combined their forces to launch an offensive to put a stop to it in 1103. Sviatopolk II had married the daughter of the Kipchak khan, which did not prevent his father-in-law from ravaging the lands of his son-in-law.

Vladimir Monomakh again penetrated into Kipchak territory in a series of victorious campaigns in 1109, 1111, 1113 and 1116, which drove the Kipchaks back southward. But none of these victories was decisive and Vladimir Monomakh concluded no fewer than twelve treaties in twelve years (1113-1125) with them. On his death, Kiev's great period came to an end. After that, the Russians were on the defensive, while the city became depopulated as large numbers of people moved to Suzdal, Vladimir, Rostov, and Moscow.

The Kipchaks had been hard hit by the campaigns of Vladimir Monomakh and fell back, some towards the Balkans, some towards the regions occupied by the Volga Bulgars.

Some of them, such as the Kipchak troops of David Aghmashenvili, an elite corps, had helped to make Georgia a very powerful kingdom. At this time (1120), the Kipchaks were to be found in the Caucasus, the Balkans, and along the Danube. Rabbi Petahia of Ratisbon,[8] who traveled through the Kipchak lands in the early twelfth century, noted that: "They have no king but only princes and (noble) families." The Galician and Volynian chronicles record that "Khan Syrchan remained [alone] on the Don where he fed himself on nothing but fish." Prince Vladimir Monomakh's campaigns had led to the withdrawal to the other side of the Caucasus of a Kipchak khan, Otrak, brother of khan Syrchan. Once settled in Abkhazia he had placed himself at the service of the ruler of Georgia:

> ...After the death of prince Vladimir Monomakh, Khan Syrchan sent his bard Oria to his brother, Khan Otrok in Abkhazia. And told him to tell him: "Vladimir is dead. Come back to your native country, brother." And he further said to Oria: "Repeat to him these words and sing him a Kipchak song and if he still refuses to come back, then let him small the scent of the herb of the steppe."[9]

> As Khan Otrok did not want to return nor to listen to the bard's songs, the bard presented him with a bouquet of herb of the steppe. When Khan Otrok inhaled the absinth scent of the herb of the steppe, he began to weep and said: "It is better to die in one's native country than win glory on foreign soil." And he returned to the steppe.

From 1068 to 1210, the pressure of the Kipchaks on Russia continued to increase all the time: they launched no fewer than fifty devastating incursions into Russian territory. Although there was no strong central authority among the Kipchaks, they proved to be better organized and were more numerous than the Pechenegs.

And so, every year, after 1125, the Russians had to face an incursion or suffer a raid. Peasants would be killed, their granaries burned, the women and children carried off into slavery. Chernigov, the second most important city after Kiev, was sacked. The Russian Bogatyri (frontier cavalry) were under continuous pressure. This was not the only threat. The Volga Bulgars attacked Riazan in 1155 but were repelled. Trade routes, by land and water, towards Constantinople were blockaded and there were too few Russians on the steppe frontiers to conduct an offensive policy, especially as there were chronic divisions among the Russians. Vladimir Monomakh's grandson, Andrew Bogoliubski (1111-1174), son of Yuri Dolgoruki and a Kipchak princess, made Vladimir his capital and sacked Kiev in 1162. His brother Vsevolod III (1176-1212), who reigned at Vladimir, launched a major offensive against the Volga Bulgars in 1183-1184.

The khan of the Kipchaks ravaged the Dniepr basin in 1184. The following year, Igor of Novgorod-Seversk set out on campaign against him and fell into his hands. Although it was a minor campaign, Igor's defeat in northern Ukraine gave rise to the epic tale known as *The Lay of the Host of Igor*.

> ...The Polovtsis have come from the other side of the Don and from the sea. They are encircling the Russian troops on all sides...

For now, brothers, a time of misfortunes has come from the steppe and overwhelmed the forces of Russia...

Neither the Russians nor the Kipchaks were capable of building enduring unity. Thus, they were in no position to deliver a decisive blow. In 1221, Mstislav, prince of Novgorod, supported by the troops of his father-in-law, the khan of the Kipchaks, drove the Poles back. But it was not long before the Mongol threat brought the Kipchaks and Russians together. They were smashed together at the battle of Kalka in 1223 by Subodei and Jebe, at the head of Mongol troops. The Kipchaks fled towards Hungary where other Kipchaks had already sought refuge and there converted to Christianity. As for Russia, it was soon almost entirely conquered by the Mongols who occupied it for more than two and a half centuries and left a lasting mark on it.

The Exception of Western Europe

Compared to the Asian or Russian fronts, Western Europe stands out as a singular exception; Attila's Huns made no more than an incursion, murderous though it was. The Avars were contained on the confines of Germany. After a series of raids at the beginning of the tenth century, the Hungarians were defeated by the emperor of Germany and were soon integrated into the West by conversion to Catholicism.

The Roman Empire and the Huns

In the second half of the fourth century A.D., the Huns, who came originally from central Asia, began to move and pushed aside first the Alans (ancestors of the Ossetians) who nomadized along the Don. The shock waves begun by the Huns over a century set off a *Völkerwanderung* that affected a series of peoples, notably Germanic ones. These, in turn, put increased pressure on the Roman empire and precipitated the fall of the Roman empire in the West.

Some of the Alans joined the Huns, who in c. 370, turned against the Ostrogoths who were occupying Ukraine, that is, the steppe between the Don and the Dniestr. The Ostrogoths were defeated and their ruler killed himself. After attacking and defeating the eastern Goths, the Huns successfully struck at the western Goths or Visigoths who fell back en masse towards Thrace (376), and, in one of those classic chain reactions, came up against the Romans. The legions of the emperor Valerian collapsed before the cavalry of the Visigoths at Adrianople in 378. The Eastern Roman empire drove them back westward. The Visigoths took Rome in 410 and finally settled as *foedarati* in Aquitaine. Meanwhile, the Huns had advanced across Caucasia into Asia Minor by way of Armenia, Syria, Palestine, and northern Mesopotamia. Their raids, on a larger scale than those directed at the west, seemed like a cataclysm in the chronicles of the sedentary peoples that had to endure them.

Saint Jerome wrote:

> Alas, messengers came running and the whole of the East trembled at the announcement of the arrival of the Huns... they filled the whole world with panic and massacres while they sped alow on their quick-moving horses.... May Jesus spare the Roman world such beasts in years to come.... They were there even before they were expected. Their speed preceded the rumour. And they took no pity on religion or rank or age...[10]

The Huns defeated the Goths in 400 and the head of the Goths' chief was sent to the Romans to obtain payment. A treaty was signed with Rome. At the beginning of the fifth century, the Huns crossed the Carpathians and poured into Pannonia. They defeated the Goths a second time in 406. In the same year, in shock waves, Vandals, Swabians, and Alans crossed the Rhine, followed by the Burgundians and the Alamans. The Huns made a devastating incursion into Thrace in 422. The Romans agreed to pay them an annual sum of three hundred and fifty pounds of gold. From China to Rome, relations between nomads and sedentary empires were much the same: to be protected by a *limes* or by a wall; use the help of allied people, or offensives with a defensive intent or temporary alliances, quest for allies in the enemy's rear, and using diplomacy to stoke tribal disputes.

After directing their attacks at the Roman empire in the east, the Huns made Hungary their base. In about 445, Attila, after his brother's murder, ensured his power over the "confederacy" of Hun tribes and, thereby, became a mortal threat to Rome. The legend of Attila does not do justice to the fact that he generally preferred political maneuver to battle and does not say that in reality by the time that the Huns attacked Western Europe, while they remained steppe nomads, they had greatly modified their habitual mode of combat based on harassment to seek shock in the manner of the Germans. Moreover, Attila's forces were largely made up of Germans and Alans. After ravaging the Balkans (444-447), they ravaged Gaul.

It was the Roman general Aetius who faced Attila's Huns on the Catalaunian plains (not far from Troyes) in 451. As a child, Aetius had been sent for three years as a hostage with the Huns. The Romans offered children as hostage in this way when they were seeking an alliance with the Huns, for example, against the Visigoths in 427 or the Burgundians in 430. Subsequently, when a Roman soldier, Aetius used Hun auxiliaries. He was familiar with their world, and no doubt with their manner of fighting. The power of the Huns had become formidable over the last decade. In Thrace, the defeated Romans had had to agree to a tribute of more than two thousand pounds of gold and to concede a no man's land of six days' march south of the Danube in favor of the Huns.

Ammianus Marcellinus,[11] the fourth-century Roman historian wrote:

> Being lightly equipped and very sudden in their movements they can deliberately scatter and gallop about at random, inflicting tremendous slaughter; their extreme nimbleness enables them to force a rampart or pillage an enemy's camp before one catches sight of them. What makes them the most formidable of all warriors is that they shoot from a distance arrows tipped with sharp splinters of bone instead of the usual heads; these are joined to the shaft with wonderful skill. At close quarters they fight without regard for their lives, and while their opponents are guarding against sword-thrusts they catch their limbs in lassos of twisted cloth which make it impossible for them to ride or walk. (Book 31)

And he added:

> They take as much delight in the dangers of war as quiet and peaceful folk in ease and leisure. They regard it as the height of good fortune to lose one's life in battle; those who grow old and die a natural death are reviled as degenerate cowards. Their proudest boast is to have killed a man, no matter whom, and their most coveted trophy is to use the flayed skins of their decapitated foes as trappings for their horses. (Book 31)

Yet the Huns behaved as a first-rate power. Already an embassy from Attila had been to Constantinople in 449 to make a protest, mingled with threats, that the legions had not withdrawn six days' march south of the Danube as had been agreed.

Attila advanced from Pannonia towards Mainz. His objective was to get rid of Aetius who commanded the main Roman army in the west of the empire. After that it would be relatively easy to crush the armies of the emperor Valentinian, if indeed Rome was Attila's final objective. Aetius was able to ensure the support of the ruler of the Visigoths, Theoderic, who was concerned about the growing power of the Huns. Aetius hastened to Orleans, which was besieged, and when he learned this Attila retreated towards the Marne, having only part of his troops before that city. He regrouped them and, with a larger cavalry force, he chose a favorable terrain on which to give battle, not far from Troyes. In reality, on both sides, most combatants were Goths fighting in their usual manner, which was not that of the nomad archers. Battle was only joined in mid-afternoon, when Aetius had secured for himself control of a hill. The Roman general entrusted the right flank to the Visigothic ruler. In the center, he had concentrated the Alan mercenaries and other auxiliaries. He himself commanded the left flank at the head of the Roman troops.

Attila, detecting the enemy's weak point, took command of the center, at the head of his best troops. On the wings, his allies, the Ostrogoths and the Gepids. Then he charged to break in the enemy's center. The center, held by the Alans, pulled back but continued fighting. But the flanks of the Roman army stood firm. In the charge the Visigothic king met his death. But Attila, seeing the danger of the pincer movement closing in on his center, retreated and took refuge behind the circle of his chariots. The Hun archers had no difficulty repulsing the assaults by the Visigoths.

The following day, Attila awaited the attack. The Romans who had themselves suffered heavily gave up the idea of attacking and let Attila withdraw. This halt was only a semi-victory, as Attila had retained his military potential. The following year, he attacked Italy, but nothing decisive happened; the leader of the Huns died in 453 and his empire rapidly disintegrated. Some Huns retreated toward Ukraine; others engaged themselves as mercenaries of the dying Roman empire. The most important result of the Hun raids was, in one of those usual chain reactions, the German drive that put an end to the Roman empire in the West. In 455, the Vandals occupied Rome. Before long, the imperial insignias were sent to Constantinople (476).

Some of the Huns had headed for Constantinople. They were defeated in Thrace by Roman troops (469). A chronicler records that the head of one of Attila's sons "was brought to Constantinople, carried in procession along the city's main artery and set on a wooden pole at the gate to the wooden circus."

During the first half of the sixth century, the upheavals that followed on the German invasions, themselves indirectly accelerated by the Hun drive, virtually ran their course. The Franks eliminated their rivals (Visigoths, Alamans, Burgundians, etc.). The Ostrogoths were decimated in Italy.

From now on, Western Europe, the small cape of Eurasia, would experience four invasions on its soil, only two of which came from central Asia, that of the Avars (late sixth-early ninth century and that of the Hungarians (tenth century). After 955, that is, the middle of the tenth century, Western Europe experienced no invasions.

The Arab invasion in the eighth century mainly affected Spain and Portugal. The incursions by the Viking sea nomads, in the ninth century (especially from 834 to 865) affected England, France (the Seine—Paris on numerous occasions, the Loire, Guyenne), Italy, Spain (Seville), and Germany (Hamburg).

Driven out of central Asia, the Avars first threatened Byzantium in the sixth century and then made a few incursions between the Elbe and the Alps (562 and 566) where they clashed without success with Sigibert, king of the Franks in Thuringia. The following year, their khaghan allied with the Lombards, and the Avars helped to crush the Gepids, another German tribe that had once been allied with Attila against Rome. Finally, the Avars successfully secured their occupation of Pannonia (568). They then turned against Byzantium, which they harassed, sometimes very dangerously, for almost a century.

But another nomad wave, the Bulgars, who also came from central Asia, drove them out of the Balkans (680). The history of the Avars after that is the history of a struggle lasting more than a century to cut a path westward. In Bavaria, they clashed with the Franks who defeated them in the middle of the eighth century. A little later, they were threatening Lombardy and, once again, Bavaria. They were again driven back by the Franks (788). They suffered two Frankish offensives, the second waged by Charlemagne on the Danube (791). The Avars were disunited and were defeated. The following year, Pippin, king of Italy, delivered them a harsh blow. The last Avar forces were destroyed by the Bulgars in Transylvania in 805. Those Avars who joined the Bulgars fought against the Byzantine empire and were annihilated in the Peloponnese. The arrival of the Hungarians in the lands along the Danube at the end of the ninth century delivered their coup de grâce.

The Hungarians (Magyars) belong to the Finno-Ugrian language group (Finland and Hungary are the two most advanced westerly outposts of the world that came originally from the steppes of Asia and/or the forests of Russia). Driven out of the steppes of Kuban by the Pechenegs, themselves pushed by another Turkic-speaking group, the Oghuz, the Hungarians reached the Danube delta at the end of the ninth century (c.880). The Byzantines took them as allies against the Bulgars. These latter called in the Pechenegs to help and they drove the Hungarians back westward (889-895) into Pannonia (Hungary). After defeating the king of Moravia, the Hungarians started to ravage the West: Italy (900), Lorraine (910-912), Burgundy and

Provence (924), Champagne (926) and again Lorraine, Champagne and Burgundy (954). The most powerful ruler in the West, Otto, the emperor of Germany, annihilated them at Lechfeld, near Augsburg in 955. Shortly after, the king of the Hungarians converted to Christianity and they would later become one of the bastions of Christendom against the Ottomans.

In the thirteenth century, the irresistible Mongol tide that had devastated Poland and Hungary and reached the Adriatic stopped abruptly on news of the death of the Great Khan. The Mongols turned round and never returned. The tip of land of Western Europe situated west of a line from Trieste to Gdansk through Vienna was overall extraordinarily preserved.

It was a singular fate, compared to that of Russia or the Balkans. Already by the middle of the tenth century, Western Europe had the privilege of no longer being the scene of invasions. Surely, this fact must be seen as one of the key features of its future destiny.

Notes

1. *Ssu-ma Ch'ien, Shi Ji*, chaps. 111 and 123.
2. At the beginning of the second century A.D., the Yüeh-Chi, under the great Buddhist ruler Kanishka, dominated the vast Kushan empire (first century B.C.-third century A.D.).
3. Traditional Chinese policy is in this respect classic, based on the formula Yiyizhiyi, "using Barbarians against Barbarians."
4. Owen Lattimore, *Inner Asian Frontiers of China* (New York: American Geographical Society, 1940).
5. They date from the eighth century and under the earliest texts in Turkish.
6. Claude Cahen, "La campagne de Manzikert d'après les sources musulmanes," *Byzantium*, IX, 2, 1934.
7. *Maurice's Strategikon. Handbook of Byzantine Military Strategy*, trans. George T. Dennis (Philadelphia: University of Pennsylvania Press, 1984).
8. *Travels of Rabbi Petachia of Ratisbon*, trans. A. Benisch (London: Trubner & Co., 1856).
9. *Artemisia absinthium*.
10. *Letters*. Saint Jerome (c.340-420) spent much of his life as a hermit in Syria-Palestine.
11. *The Later Roman Empire (344-378)*, Books 14-31, trans. Walter Hamilton (Harmondsworth: Penguin, 1986).

3

The Apogee of the Nomads:
Mongols and Turkic-Speakers
(Thirteenth-Fifteenth Centuries)

The Mongols

The rise to power of Genghis Khan, deprived of protection at a very early age by the death of his father, was difficult and slow. He was born between 1155 and 1167, about 1165, and became khan of the Mongols in 1197, according to his most penetrating biographer, Paul Ratchnevsky.[1] It took him ten years of hard political struggles and wars (1196-1206) to subdue the tribal confederacies that made up those whom we call Mongols and who were known to European history in the Middle Ages as Tartars: Naimans—who were Nestorian Christians—Keraits recently converted to Christianity, Merkites, Tatars, and Oirats, these last three, like the Mongols, adepts of Shamanism. Traditionally, the confederacies of tribes coming together to make war were loosely structured and rather unstable, and would rapidly disintegrate, with each tribe clinging to its own interests.

It was only when he was past forty at the very least that Genghis, or Temuchin as he was then known, became the leader of the "peoples who live under tents." It was then that the grand assembly of notables, which took major decisions—the *khuriltai*—proclaimed him supreme leader: Genghis Khan.

Until the thirteenth century, compared to the Turkic-speaking peoples, the Mongols had played a relatively secondary role in High Asia. During the two previous centuries, they had driven the Kirghiz out of Mongolia, but they lacked unity and had not yet created an empire. Power was shared among aristocratic families, with a hierarchy comprising knights (*bahadur*), princes or tribal leaders (*noyons*), wise men (*setsen*), *khans*, and the supreme khan (*ka-khan*). The

59

warriors (*nokur*) were free men. The serfs were members of defeated clans.

Among the Mongols, as among all the nomad peoples who preceded them, disunity and conflict prevailed until Genghis Khan subjected them to a common discipline. The tribes were in latent conflict or open war.

According to the same decimal principle as was used for the army, Genghis Khan divided the Mongols as a people into family units (ten, a hundred, a thousand families). This was a system that the Golden Horde later applied to Russia. Once assigned to a given unit, any individual who left it risked the death penalty.

In the thirteenth century, Mongolia was prosperous. It was not hungry nomads or nomads being pressed from behind by other groups who set off on campaigns but a rising power seeking to expand. In the beginning, the Mongols had no administrative structure; the whole enterprise depended on the organizational and political genius of an extraordinary nomad who pursued a patient and relentless strategy, and thereby succeeded in rising to the top after he had eliminated his rivals.

At the time that Genghis Khan attained power, the world could be broadly divided into three parts:

There was *China*, itself divided: in the south, the Sung dynasty, prosperous and formidable since it had been fighting off conquest for four decades; in the north, a dynasty founded by nomads of Tungus/Manchu origin who had seized power in the previous century after defeating the Liao dynasty (itself a sinicized dynasty, the Khitans); in the north-west, the Tanguts or Xia-Xia (a dynasty founded by Buddhist Tibetans). China was without any doubt the major focus of Mongol designs and proved to be the toughest of adversaries.

Islam, for its part, had been disunited for several centuries. The Seljukids of Iran had disappeared in 1157 and they were weakened in Asia Minor, the impact of the Crusades still being felt. The Seljukids were surrounded by the Crusaders, Byzantium—itself much weakened—and the Qara Khitaï (who were Buddhist). On the ruins of what had been the Seljukid empire of Iran, the state of Khorezm, with its capital at Samarqand, had arisen just a few decades before the arrival of Genghis Khan, and extended as far as the confines of India; its population was predominantly Iranian. At the head of this extensive empire was Ala al-din Mohamed II, whose still somewhat tenuous hold on power rested on a rather unreliable mercenary army.

Further away, the *Christian world*—Orthodox or Catholic—was also disunited, with, in the West, a papacy that was unable to unite it, indeed was rather doing the opposite, for as the thirteenth century opened, the struggle between the pope and the Holy Roman Empire was at its height. As the Mongol threat drew closer, the Swedes, together with the Knights Templar and the Teutonic Knights, were fighting the Orthodox and advancing on Novgorod.

Genghis Khan's prime concern was to avoid tribal cabals, which might undermine his power. He sought to win loyalty by favoring the promotion of war chiefs of humble origins who owed him everything. He tried to break down tribal bonds by instituting intertribal units bound together by very strict discipline, and by removing combatants from their home areas. Building on the traditions of the steppe, he instituted a code that was partly already in existence and partly new, the *Yasa*. The administration that he set up remained the model for all nomad societies over the centuries that followed. He utilized the existing decimal system, typical of the steppe, but succeeded in creating troops with a discipline previously unseen in the steppe and unrivaled in medieval or ancient history. For his chancery this unlettered nomad caused the Uighur script to be used. He very quickly learned to draw on the know-how of the Chinese and the Persians.

In order to limit tribal solidarities, Genghis Khan created an imperial guard (*keshig*), which had ten thousand men; it included both elite elements, whatever their social background, and members of noble families, which might be interpreted as hostage-taking. Above all, the guard constituted the core of those loyal to the regime instituted by Genghis Khan.

The pursuit of hunting was the nomads' military academy. It took place on horseback using the bow, as in war, and the battues, for the great hunts, involved the whole army, until a large circle gradually closed in around the prey. Every man was liable to military service up to the age of sixty. There was no distinction between combatants and non-combatants. There were only elite combatants and the rest, almost all remarkable for their endurance and the accuracy of their shooting. The major weapon, at least at the beginning of engagements, was the double-curved bow, typical of nomads.

Genghis Khan's conquests were made gradually. First, he ensured control of the steppe and the forest zones bordering on it. The Kirghiz on the upper Yenisei and the Oirots around Lake Baikal made their submission (1207). Two years later, the Uighurs acknowledged that they were vassals of Genghis Khan; on the Ordos, the Tanguts (state of Xia-Xia) submitted. Everything impelled the Mongols to conquer China: geography and the immemorial fascination of nomads for the rich and prestigious sedentary state whose rulers would grant honorific titles to nomads. The Mongols had little difficulty in getting past (or round) the walls and ravaged the state of Chin, ruled by the Jurchens. But they lacked siege equipment and were unable to take the cities (1211). The revolt of the Khitaï (Khitans), formerly masters of northern China, against their Chin (Jurchen) masters and their switch to the Mongol side changed everything. Thanks to Khitan civil and military engineers and cadres, the Mongols were able to acquire the know-how they lacked (1212). This first campaign in China was more like a raid. An armistice was negotiated with the Chin; Genghis married one of the emperor's daughters. But the Chin evacuated their capital, Beijing, and fell back towards Kaifeng. At once, the Mongols seized Beijing and sacked it. Genghis withdrew from China. The conquest was still not complete by 1216, but he entrusted it to one of his most outstanding generals and one who had risen from the ranks, Mukali. Initially, the gap between conquering nomads and subjugated sedentary people remained stark, except for those among the sedentary people whose know-how the nomads used.

The following offensive focused on Khorezm. It was preceded by the annexation of the empire of the Qara Khitaï. At the *Kulturay* of 1218, where the *Yasa* or code of Genghis Khan was proclaimed, taking up and completing a series of rules and prohibitions,[2] the decision was taken to attack Khorezm in retaliation for the execution of Mongol envoys.

All the campaigns of Genghis Khan were waged after solid preparation. Spies were sent to collect information, spread rumors, reassure the population about religious freedom, and reconnoitre the ground. These aspects were never neglected by the Mongols under Genghis Khan. In the space of four months, he defeated what were certainly the larger forces of the shah of Khorezm (perhaps one hundred and fifty thousand against one hundred thousand Mongols), in a remarkable campaign. Faced with an adversary who had dispersed his forces along the defensive line of the Syr-Daria, Genghis Khan deceived him with a combined offensive, leaving the shah unable to determine where its center of gravity was. While two Mongol armies, one coming from the north, one from the east, headed, the first towards Samarqand, the second towards Tashkent, a third one led by Genghis Khan himself and Subodei crossed the Kizil-kum desert and burst unexpectedly on Bukhara and the rear of the shah's forces.

Such was the surprise that the shah withdrew rather than face the Mongols. Bukhara surrendered in March 1220 and the three Mongol armies converged on Samarqand.

Mobility, surprise, capacity to concentrate after a long-distance maneuver: the Khorezm campaign was a model of the genre.[3] When the defeated enemies were not simply massacred, they were reduced into slavery and distributed to military commanders who would use them as auxiliaries.

The following year, the Mongols took the city of Urgench after an extremely difficult siege, and all the inhabitants were put to the sword. Meanwhile, Genghis had sent Subodei and Jebe in pursuit of the shah. Although he was being hunted down, in the end he died without having been caught. The shah's son proved to have more fight in him. But Genghis pursued him; he crossed eastern Khorasan, which he sacked (Merv, Balkh). In this torment, a small Turkic tribe fled westward where it was granted land by the Seljukids and settled in Asia Minor. The leader of that tribe was the father of Osman, the initially very modest founder of what would become the formidable Ottoman empire. Genghis annihilated the son of the shah of Khorezm's army on the banks of the Indus in November 1221, but, after putting up a brave fight, its leader managed to escape. On their way back, the Mongols ravaged western Afghanistan (Herat, Ghazni) and eastern Iran. Genghis returned to Mongolia through what is now Kazakhstan (1225).

Meanwhile, an extraordinary cavalry raid was made towards the Caucasus, southern Russia, and back to Mongolia by Subodei and Jebe. They ravaged Azerbaijan, Georgia, and Armenia and clashed victoriously with the Kipchaks (Polovtsis) who called on the Russian princes for help. After a sham retreat by the Mongols that enabled them to split the Russians and Kipchaks into several parts, these latter were defeated at the battle of the river Kalka in 1222.

Genghis Khan's last campaign was directed against the Tanguts in north-western China, who had not been completely subdued (1227). There can be no doubt that he felt and was quite aware that he was creating a universal empire and that he wanted it to survive. When Genghis Khan died in 1227, he had already decided who would succeed him. The issue of dynastic descent, in the absence of primogeniture, remained a potent source of conflict among the nomads. There were very few nomad dynasties that had been able to survive more than two generations without dynastic conflict and the empire splitting. Uncles and brothers of the dead khan could traditionally lay claim to succeed him. The sons could legitimately do so, too: both the elder and the younger who received the wives and serving women of his father as an inheritance (except for his own mother). At the death of Genghis, the Mongol empire covered the whole of High Asia, the north of Iran and Afghanistan as well as northern China. According to his will, his empire came nominally under the Great Khan, his son Ogedei, but it was divided in the traditional manner among his sons. Ogedei inherited Zungharia, Chagatai Transoxiana, Jochi the west of the empire, and the youngest son, Tolui, according to custom, received the bulk of the troops and Mongolia, that had initially belonged to his father. The empire was united by a single code, the *Yasa*, which strengthened custom (*Yosun*), a single postal system, the *yam*, with staging posts with horses and food every fifty kilometers, making it possible for a courier to cover two to three hundred kilometers a day, and a single taxation system and, with Ogedei, and then Guyuk and Möngke, it succeeded in staying united until the death of Möngke in 1259.

The major instrument of conquest was, of course, the remarkable military machine forged by Genghis Khan, although in its early days it did not have it all its own way: Mongol detachments were defeated by the shah of Khorezm's son, etc. The Mongols, like other nomads, exterminated those who resisted them and caused them losses. Those who surrendered were spared but reduced to slavery and often used in the front line during later sieges. The only categories that were systematically spared were craftsmen and, sometimes, clerics. The Mongols made no tactical innovations: sham flight, flanking maneuvers, attrition, and disorientation through the use of arrows were all perfectly conventional tactics among nomads. In addition, in the initial battles, in the steppe, against other nomads, the Mongols also met with setbacks. In the thirteenth century, their superiority lay in innovations introduced by Genghis: breaking the other tribal chiefs in the course of a long, hard struggle, depriving traditional chiefs of their clients, promoting to positions of responsibility people who had risen from the ranks and owed him everything. This open recruitment brought to the top not only the best but also, in principle, the most loyal lieutenants. Finally, the discipline instituted by the *yasa* and Genghis' iron grip certainly gave Mongol troops an unrivaled esprit de corps and cohesion, especially compared to the armies of medieval Europe. Not only was discipline rigorous, it affected everybody, whatever his rank (except for Genghis' family). In peace time, theft or pillage were punished with death so as to avoid intertribal vendettas and protect trade, which was a profitable activity for the Mongols. The same concern to reduce the causes of conflict led to adultery being punished (among Mongols) by the death of both the man and the woman involved. On the other hand, adultery with a woman from a foreign tribe was tolerated.

Before every campaign, the Mongols took care to use psychological preparation, not only through the use of terror, but by presenting themselves as liberators. The Muslims of the Abbassid caliphate were grateful that the Mongols firmly undertook to liquidate the Assassin sect. The Eastern Christians saw the Mongols as potential allies who would strike at their Muslim opponents. The king of Armenia, who had taken good care to form an alliance with the Mongols, placed his troops at their disposal against Muslim Syria (1259). While it took less than four months to encompass the fall of Khorezm, and just a few more months for the campaign to reach the Indus, the conquest of China proved to be altogether a more arduous affair. It took a quarter of a century of struggle for the Mongols to subdue it.

The Military Organization of the Mongols under Genghis

As among the other nomads of High Asia, the organization of the army was decimal. The largest unit was the *tumen*, equivalent to a division: 10,000 men in principle (and sometimes less). An army was made up of two to four *tumen*, each composed of ten times a thousand men (the equivalent of a regiment), and each regiment of ten times a hundred men (the equivalent of a squadron), ten times ten men.

10 men	=	1 arban
100 men	=	1 jagun
1,000 men	=	1 minghan
10,000 men	=	1 tumen

At the top of this organization, where command positions were assigned by Genghis more on the basis of merit than the prestige of birth was the imperial tumen, wholly devoted to the khan and enjoying a privileged status. The generals who had risen from the ranks stood out as the most remarkable ones in Genghis Khan's army: Mukali, on the Chinese front, Subodei and Jebe on the western fronts of Khorezm and Russia.

Strong, frugal,[4] used to riding a horse from his earliest childhood—on small hardy thickset horses—and hunting from childhood, the Mongol fighter, tempered by a climate that is very harsh in both winter and summer, was doubtless superior to the other nomad fighters because of the discipline and group cohesion instituted by Genghis Khan. But this harsh discipline was in many respects egalitarian: the men received the same food as their superiors. Officers were not allowed to treat ordinary soldiers harshly except for very serious reasons. Finally, Genghis was not only victorious for military reasons but also because of his qualities as an organizer and a diplomat and his political genius, which enabled him to exploit his adversary's weaknesses. From the time of his struggles with other tribes for pre-eminence in the steppes, Genghis put about the story that the Sky had designated him to lead; throughout his conquests he caused rumors to be put about by merchants (real or disguised) to divide, sow discord, create panic, or reassure and win over malcontents.

John of Plano Carpino, an Italian Franciscan monk sent as ambassador extraordinare by Pope Innocent IV, who stayed at Karakorum in 1246, wrote:

> When they are in battle, if one or two or three or even more out of a group of ten run away, all are put to death; and if a whole group of ten flees, the rest of the group of a hundred are all put to death, if they do not flee too. In a word, unless they retreat in a body, all who take flight are put to death. Likewise if one or two or more go forward boldly to the fight, then the rest of the ten are put to death if they do not follow and, if one or more of the ten are captured, their companions are put to death if they do not rescue them.

As for their manner of fighting:

> It should be known that when they come in sight of the enemy they attack at once, each one shooting three or four arrows at their adversaries; if they see that they are not going to be able to defeat them, they retire, going back to their own line. They do this as a blind to make the enemy follow them as far as the places where they have prepared ambushes. If the enemy pursues them to these ambushes, they surround and wound and kill them. Similarly if they see that they are opposed by a large army, they sometimes turn aside and, putting a day's or two days' journey between them, they attack and pillage another part of the country and they kill men and destroy and lay waste the land. If they perceive that they cannot even do this, then they retreat for some ten or twelve days and stay in a safe place until the army of the enemy has disbanded, whereupon they come secretly

and ravage the whole land. They are indeed the most cunning in war, for they have now been fighting against other nations for forty years and more.

When however they are going to join battle, they draw up all the battle lines just as they are to fight. The chiefs or the princes of the army do not take part in the fighting but take up their stand some distance away facing the enemy, and they have beside them their children on horseback and their womenfolk and horses; and sometimes they make figures of men and set them on horses. They do this to give the impression that a great crowd of fighting-men is assembled there. They send a detachment of captives and men of other nationalities who are fighting with them to meet the enemy head-on, and some Tartars may perhaps accompany them. Other columns of stronger men they dispatch far off to the right and to the left so that they are not seen by the enemy and in this way they surround them and close in and so the fighting begins from all sides. Sometimes when they are few in number they are thought by the enemy, who are surrounded, to be many, especially when the latter catch sight of the children, women, horses and dummy figures described above, which are with the chief or prince of the army and which they think are combatants; and alarmed by this they are thrown into disorder. If it happens that the enemy fight well, the Tartars make a way of escape for them; then as soon as they begin to take flight and are separated from each other they fall upon them and more are slaughtered in flight than could be killed in battle. However, it should be known that, if they can avoid it, the Tartars do not like to fight hand to hand but they wound and kill men and horses with their arrows; they only come to close quarters when men and horses have been weakened by arrows.

The Mongol mounted archer had three or four remount horses and sometimes more. These horses rarely stood more than 1.30 meters high; they could withstand the rigorous temperatures of the Mongol winter and could cover a hundred kilometers a day on average, whatever the season. Each warrior had two bows, one long, the other short, to shoot on horseback or on foot, and two types of arrow: one to travel far and the other with powerful piercing potential. The range of the Mongol bow is said to have been two to three hundred meters, and each warrior had between sixty and eighty arrows in his quiver. The heavy cavalry, John of Plano Carpino informs us, had a lance with a hook to drag a man from his saddle, and cuirasses made of plates. The light cavalry was composed of archers. The infantry—for there was an infantry—had shields, swords, and axes.

As was usually the case among nomads, the army included all fit males between fifteen and sixty years old. It was divided into two wings and a center in the traditional pattern, with the imperial guard holding itself behind the center, ready to intervene if needed.

Battle formation was planned in this way: two ranks in front of heavy cavalry, composed of groups of a hundred men separated from one another by distinct gaps. Horses caparisoned, horsemen wearing their cuirasses with lances, clubs, and swords. Three rows of light mounted archers.

When battle was joined, the center of the three rows of mounted archers passed through the gaps left by the heavy cavalry. The wings of the light cavalry tried to take the adversary in a pincer movement, and the whole of this formation showered the enemy cavalry with arrows.

The aim was to throw the enemy off balance by decimating him. All these movements were carried out in silence. Orders were given by white or black flags that were raised or lowered. Burning torches replaced flags in night fighting. Once confusion had been sown among the enemy, the drums were beaten announcing the charge. The light cavalry fell back behind the rows of heavy cavalry to take the enemy in a pincer again soon after. The frontal attack was accompanied by harassment by the light cavalry on the enemy's flanks and rear to increase the confusion and disorder. The commander of major formations (tumen, etc.) did not fight, but controlled operations. An enemy was never wholly encircled. He always had the possibility of escape. And it was then that the Mongols proceeded, at least cost, to annihilate him. In flight, the adversary was totally vulnerable. Thus, pursuits, should they prove necessary, might often last several days. The Great Khan's guard, held in reserve, was intended to deliver the decisive blow or repel a dangerous counter-attack.

When confronted with a force that was superior in numbers or particularly strong, the Mongols used a strategy that succeeded with them again and again: they feigned flight so as to divide the enemy troops, some of whom would be mobile, some less so. Thus, Jebe and Subodei retreated for nine days in 1222 before the forces of the prince of Galish and the Kipchaks who, though better mounted than those of the Russian princes, were annihilated when the Mongols suddenly about-faced. Then the second wave of Russian horsemen was, in turn, annihilated.

Thanks to their system of plentiful remounts, the Mongols advanced or retreated faster than their adversaries. Rarely was a Mongol unit—and even more rarely an army—taken by surprise. As success followed success, over the years, their morale rose ever higher and they began to see themselves as invincible. Genghis set the objectives. But execution on the ground and in light of circumstances lay wholly with his generals. While command of the army fell on

Genghis' sons, strategy was defined by the generals who had risen from the ranks and shown their worth (Subodei, Jebe, Mukali).

In the beginning, the Mongols, being inexperienced in the art of siege warfare, were incapable of taking cities. Such was the case during their first attack on China in 1209. But, two years later, they had Chinese siege machine experts and, over the decades, they would improve them. In 1273, Khubilai received *trébuchets* from his cousin the ilkhan of Persia—catapults capable of projecting rocks weighing up to seventy kilograms with considerable force.

The Mongols also borrowed much from the Sung. They used burning arrows and pots of naphtha launched by catapult. And they used hostages to make the initial attack. Finally, the Mongols used foreign troops as auxiliaries, notably Chinese ones for the infantry and Persian ones for garrisons.

The Heirs of Genghis Khan

After the death of Genghis Khan and the election of his third son Ogedei as khan by the *khuriltai* in 1229, the second phase of conquest began. The capital of the empire was at Karakorum and the Mongols already had the embryo of a Chinese-style administration entrusted to sedentary people. From now on, conquest was no longer thought of in terms of immediate pillage but of long-term exploitation. The Chinese front was initially the key focus: reconquering the Chin empire and destroying the capital, Kaifeng (1232). Happy to be able to be rid of the Chin, the Chinese of the Sung empire helped the Mongols to crush the common enemy (1234), without appreciating the future danger.

The khuriltai of the following year decided on an offensive in every direction at once: west with Subodei, China with Mukali, Korea and the Middle East. The toughest of these fronts was southern China. Conquest of it began under the aegis of khan Ogedei and ended under Khubilai; it lasted more than forty years (1236-1279). The first attack on Korea was made victoriously between 1236 and 1241.

We know more about the western offensive and it concerns us more for several reasons.

On this front, real command belonged to Subodei, under the nominal authority of Batu, son of Jochi, Genghis Khan's eldest son. Guyuk and Kadan, sons of Ogedei, third son of Genghis Khan, Möngke, son of Tolui, Genghis Khan's youngest son, and Baïder and Böri, respectively son and grandson of Chagatai, also took part.

They set out in the autumn, the horses well fed and in good shape, in three columns: the western front army may well have numbered a hundred thousand men. The target of the northern flank was to destroy the Volga Bulgars. The southern flank was to attack the Kipchaks. These were defeated and some of them fled towards Hungary (1239).

Batu attacked the prosperous principalities of northern Russia, while southern Russia was ravaged. In December 1237, Riazan (on the river Oka) was taken and razed. "No eye was left open to weep for the dead," says the chronicle. Moscow, which at that time was just a small town, was destroyed. Vladimir was sacked (February 1238). Unlike other invaders who were victims of the Russian cold, the Mongols waged a winter campaign. Not only is the Russian climate no harsher than the climate they were familiar with at home, but the frozen rivers could be crossed on horseback with no need to worry about knowing whether the bridges had been destroyed.

The encounter with the Russian army took place in March 1238, and, after a battle lasting two days, it was crushingly defeated not far from the river Sit. The city of Novgorod, as well as Pskov and a number of others, escaped the common fate, as the thaw rendered the terrain increasingly impracticable. Alexander Nevsky, who had defeated the Swedes in 1240 and the Teutonic Knights in 1242, understood that it was pointless to put up any resistance to the Mongols. He decided to pay the tribute imposed and saved Novgorod from being sacked.

In the south, the following year, Batu linked up with Möngke and they spent part of the year resting and pasturing the horses. Meanwhile, Armenia had been ravaged in 1239, and in 1240 operations resumed: Ukraine was pillaged and its cities, Ternigov and Kiev were taken and burned.

At the beginning of 1241, the Mongols, led by Subodei and Batu, turned towards Hungary. The army was divided into four columns, each containing perhaps twenty or twenty-five thousand men. One of them, commanded by Kaidu, was first sent towards Sandomir, on the Vistula (March 1241) and then, two or three tumens strong, met two Polish armies at Szydlow, defeated them both (18 March) and took Cracow and Breslau.

Commanded by the duke of Silesia, the Teutonic Knights went to meet the Mongols with the support of the Templars and the Knights

Hospitaller and Polish contingents. Although inferior in number, the Mongols won an overwhelming victory at Leignitz. The king of Bohemia, who had not been able to come to the aid of the duke of Silesia's troops, tried vainly to operate a belated link-up with the Hungarian forces.

Meanwhile, Subodei had advanced with three columns towards Hungary. The flanks set off first, while, in the center, Subodei himself started out a little later so that the three columns should converge together on Gran, the Hungarian capital. The column advancing to the north skirted the Carpathians and then turned back towards the forces of the central column headed by Subodei. The southern column passing through Transylvania also turned back. The central column advancing fast along the valley of the Theiss reached the Danube not far from Gran. The three columns met up on 4 April 1241. On the other side of the Danube, the troops of King Bela of Hungary are estimated to have numbered some one hundred thousand men.

Subodei refused to take the risk of crossing the Danube, and then having to fight with his back to the river, and feigned a slow retreat, which lasted over a week, drawing the Hungarian army after him. On 10 April 1241, while the two armies were separated by the river Sajo, Subodei crossed the river by night, and surprised his adversary just as dawn broke. Batu, who had secured control of the sole bridge, launched a frontal attack while Subodei forded the river further up and surprised the army of the king of Hungary from the rear, cutting it to pieces before mid-day, as it beat a retreat. Two-thirds of the Hungarian army was put out of action. At Gran, the Mongols had defeated the Hungarian army along with German, French, and Croat contingents, as well as the Templars.

The power of medieval armies in the West in the thirteenth century (the crossbow only appeared in the fourteenth century) lay wholly in the shock power of the heavy cavalry. If it did not have the possibility of charging, a medieval army had nothing to fall back on.

With Hungary occupied, a reconnaissance mission was sent out into Austria and Croatia as far as the Dalmatian coast. News of the death of khan Ogedei in Karakorum brought the Mongol troops back to the capital, so that Batu could be present at the khuriltai.

In 1242, the Mongols defeated the Seljukid sultanate of Rum. They destroyed Erzerum. The following year, with thirty thousand men, Batu totally defeated a Seljukid army of eighty thousand men at

Kuzadag, eighty kilometers east of Sivas. Then Sivas and Caesarea were taken. The sultanate never recovered from the Mongol invasion.

With the exception of Iran and southern China, the empire had reached its greatest peak in the mid-thirteenth century, in just forty years,

**

After the death of Genghis, when the four sons of his first wife succeeded him, the empire experienced several crisis-free decades. Under Ogedei, the conquests continued. On his death, the succession took a long time to settle. There was an interregnum (1242-1246) during which the Seljukids of Rum were crushed near Erzinjan (1243). The sultan acknowledged Mongol suzerainty.

Less then twenty years elapsed between the death of Ogedei and the reign of Khubilai, the last of the great khans. Guyuk and Möngke reigned in the intervening period. The former was a son of Ogedei, the latter a son of Tolui, Genghis's youngest son supported by Batu. Guyuk was elected at the khuriltai of 1246, Möngke in 1251. During this period, the Mongols remained more or less neutral in religious disputes, although they tended to favor the Nestorians. The descendants of Tolui, the youngest son, stood out: after producing Möngke, great khan 1251-1259, they produced Khubilai, great khan 1260-1294, the founder of the Yuan dynasty which reigned for a century in China, and Hulagu who founded the dynasty of the ilkhans of Iran. This latter put down the Ismailis of the Assassin Order and took their stronghold of Alamut; then, in 1258, he took Baghdad, which he sacked for over two weeks. In 1260, Hulagu, who favored the Nestorians, took Damascus with his Christian allies, who included the Nestorian general Kit-Buqa, the Norman crusader leader Bohemond of Taranto, and the Armenian king of Cilicia, Hetum I. Hetum had been to Karakorum in 1254-1255 where, in agreement with the papacy, he had sought to make an alliance with the Mongols to attack Islam from the rear.

In the same year, the Mongols, or at least a small band of them, suffered a defeat at the hands of the Mamluks at Aïn Jalut in Syria. The Mamluks were soldiers who were former slaves, often Turkish-speaking, employed in Egypt. They seized power in 1250 and concerned themselves principally with military organization, leaving the business of administration in the hands of the Egyptians. They made formidable adversaries, equipped as they were with a rapid intelligence service and combat tactics very similar to those of the Mongols and other nomad peoples. Their victory at Aïn Jalut put a halt to Mongol expansion along the Syrian-Palestinian corridor, which in any event was hardly suited to feed a large cavalry force.[5] But it is noteworthy that after Aïn Jalut, the Mamluks made no attempt to go on the attack. In the thirteenth century, Mongol power was unchallenged.

On the death of Möngke, his two brothers Khubilai and Böke claimed the title of great khan. The latter, as the younger son, was ruler of the Mongol homeland. He was supported by Chagatai (central Asia) and Bereke (leader of the Ulus of Jochi). Khubilai, backed by the Mongol army, engaged in the conquest of Sung China; he enjoyed the support of Hulagu, the ilkhan ruler of Iran. Khubilai emerged victor. He transferred the Mongol capital from Karakorum to Beijing.

After a long struggle, Sung China was conquered (1271). Khubilai joined Yunnan to the provinces of China and founded the Yuan dynasty, which reigned for ninety years. The north was firmly held against incursions. The Mongols who had conquered Korea (1272) tried in vain to land in Japan (1281) and then tried again with a large fleet (1281). A typhoon (*kamikaze*) destroyed the fleet in port and saved Japan. But, in 1293, the Mongols succeeded in landing in Java.

While the Mongols suffered a setback in Annam against the Vietnamese, they were victorious in Cambodia (1296), and Burma after a hard-fought struggle (1297).

While Khubilai and Arik Böke quarreled over who was to inherit power, in the west another power struggle was unfolding which was complicated by religious divergences. The ethnic make-up of the Golden Horde was becoming increasingly Turkic, but what was more important is that khan Berke, Batu's brother, converted to Islam. He declared that religious ties were stronger than blood ties and allied with the Mamluks against Hulagu, ilkhan of Persia, protector of the Nestorian Christians. Berke inflicted a defeat on Hulagu (1264). Hulagu died the following year, but the struggle between the Golden Horde, which had embraced Islam, and the ilkhanate of Iran went on until the end of the thirteenth century.

The fact is that by 1264 the Mongol empire was united in name only. It was made up of more or less federated states whose divergent interests were sharpened by conflicts that had their roots in religion.

The proclamation of religious freedom was valuable politically. By asserting it, Genghis Khan avoided conflicts among Muslims becoming transformed into a holy war and reassured the other religions. Subsequently, Ogedei, Guyuk, and Möngke met representatives of many religions—Christians, Buddhists, Muslims and Taoists—but the Mongols lacked the zeal of those who wanted to convert others to revelation and retained until their own conversion an open attitude towards the religions of the defeated.[6]

In Turkestan, the Chagatai became Turkified and also converted to Islam. At the other end of the empire, the great khan Khubilai opted for Buddhism (c. 1264). The initial tolerance observed for political reasons and above all out of indifference to the problem of proselytism was over. From now on, Muslims, like Buddhists, would seek zealously to spread and impose what they felt to be the true faith.

The ilkhans of Persia converted to Islam under Gazan (1295) and he ordered the destruction of every Buddhist temple, every church, and every synagogue. The Christians were massacred. A few years later, Uzbek, khan of the Golden Horde, embraced Islam and imposed it on the Horde. In short, apart from China and Mongolia proper, the western part of the empire became Turkified and Islamic and it was increasingly sharply divided among the ilkhanate of Iran, the Golden Horde, and the Chagatai, while the influence of Persian culture was highly visible all over the area.

In two generations, everything had changed. Division was a fact. The conquering nomads had adopted the religion of those they had subdued and, generally, their culture. In China, the sedentary peoples, thanks to their knowledge, occupied an ever-more important place in the bureaucratic management of the state, while the Mongols became sinicized. But, until the death of Khubilai (1294), nominally, his power was recognized as supreme throughout the Mongol empire. The empire enjoyed over a quarter of a century of peace (1280-1307), until the death of Khubilai's grandson, who was his successor on the throne of the Yuan.

In the fourteenth century, the khanates of China and Persia—countries with the greatest cultural depth—were the first to collapse.

As might be logically expected, the empire of the Mongols survived longest in the traditional area of nomad empires—the Eurasian steppe, from Mongolia through Turkestan to southern Russia. The descendants of Jochi and Chagatai, masters of central Asia and Russia, retained their power longest.

This conquest society reached its zenith in the mid-fourteenth century. Then the fissiparous forces won the day. The cultures of the old civilizations played their integrating role, first and foremost in the religious sphere. And they did so all the more because the conquerors were few in number and their religious ideology quite clearly was no match for the spiritual depth of more developed religions.

The Turkic-Speakers

Timur

Timur Leng (Tamerlane) Timur, known as the lame (1336-1405), was a Muslim Turk from the Ulus of Chagatai who saw himself as Genghis Khan's heir. He was a military genius, steeped in Persian culture, who created a vast empire of which the jewel was Samarqand, and his action appears, unavoidably, as a less successful repetition of the epic of Genghis Khan. Not only was Genghis Khan the first to create such a large empire, but he had succeeded in establishing an enduring legitimacy and, in his life-time, compelling tribal society to bend to the laws of the *Yasa*, while promoting innovative military talents.

Timur's historic role must be assessed both in relation to the heritage of Genghis Khan, whom he sought to emulate and which he strengthened even as he reduced the impact of the Mongols, and in relation to Islam. In this respect, he took advantage of two vacuums. Since 1258, there had been no longer a caliph in Baghdad; the caliphate was held by the Mamluks of Egypt. Since 1294, there had been no great khan. Timur proclaimed himself emir, but reigned maintaining the fiction that he held power from the Genghiskhanids. As a Muslim, he ensured the removal of everything that was not Islamic (Christianity, Buddhism, etc.) while retaining Genghis Khan's *Yasa*, even those parts which might be seen as contradicting Islam. His troops were essentially Turkish-speaking and had only recently become sedentary; he saw his wars as holy wars, even though most of his wars were with other Muslims. But in Persia, Iraq, and northern India he relied on the principle of Islamic legitimacy. His empire was enormous: from the marshes of Sinkiang to Anatolia and from Transoxiana to the Indus. But it was modest in size compared to that of the Mongols a century earlier.

Timur is often regarded as the last of the great nomad conquerors. But that judgment is unfair, measured by the yardstick of the consequences of a conquest. At least, Babur, the conqueror of northern

India (1526) and founder of the dynasty of the great Mughals, who reigned over virtually the whole Indian sub-continent for over two centuries, must be added.

Timur raised himself to power slowly. As in every tribal group where the leader is not totally legitimate, the rise to power is very difficult and repeatedly contested. Timur took ten years to assert his leadership over the Ulus of Chagatai, from his own Barlas tribe. Creating loyalty to his person took care and it took time. All through his career as a conqueror, a quarter of a century for the period of expansion (1379-1405), Timur continually kept his army and his subordinates busy in remote campaigns. He created provincial armies to divide the members of a single family by assigning them to remote regions. He kept close to him the most powerful figures, they being the least reliable ones. Above all, he poured favors on the princes who owed him everything. Like every ruler anxious to create a new order, he encouraged the formation of new elites.

All of Timur's military undertakings were successes. He experienced no defeat on the field of battle, although it is true that, unlike Genghis, he several times had to start the conquest of this or that area all over again or face an adversary he had once defeated a second or third time.

The reason, undoubtedly, is that in the interim the world had changed and the states around Transoxiana, his rear base, were more powerful than they had been before.

Timur's Victories

1379	Conquest of Khorezm
1380-1381	Conquest of Iran
1386	Conquest of Iraq and Azerbaijan
1387	First victory over Tuqtamish and the Golden Horde
1391	New victory over Tuqtamish
1395	Final victory over Tuqtamish
1398	Capture of Delhi
1400-1401	Capture of Aleppo and Damascus. Victory over the Mamluks
1401	Sack of Baghdad
1402	Victory over Bayazid and the Ottomans near Ankara
1404-1405	Departure for the conquest of China. Dies on the way.

What was special about Timur? He was a Muslim, came from a Turkish-speaking group that was Persian by culture, but his political legitimacy was of Mongol origin (*yasa*). The backbone of his army was made up of recently sedentarized people, mostly from the Chagatai khanate. The world that he conquered was not, as it had been for Genghis Khan, a foreign world, but a known world. Moreover, Timur reigned not over the steppe but mostly over Asia south of Transoxiana, although his capital was Samarqand.

His most tenacious adversary was the Golden Horde, led by Tuqtamish, skilled in all the tactics of the nomads and having remarkable war-hardened troops at his disposal. To conquer him took all of Timur's tenacity, combined with his military genius. "I stay with what I am doing. Once a project had captured my attention, whatever it might be, I gave it all my attention and I would never abandon it until I had succeeded in it," wrote Timur in the *Institutes* or *Twelve Rules of Behaviour* that are attributed to him. It did indeed take a great deal of constancy to track down, through several extended campaigns, an adversary who practiced a scorched earth policy while at the same time harassing the conqueror's forces. Tuqtamish was no small adversary. He, too, nurtured the ambition of restoring the empire of Genghis Khan.

Later, before Delhi, Timur had to deal with his Indian adversary's elephants, which terrified his troops and initially forced them to withdraw. Timur then had ditches dug, which acted as traps, and, in addition, had buffaloes let loose with flaming faggots burning on their backs; the maddened animals sowed terror among the elephants while his cavalry strewed sharp-pointed trivets in front of the elephants.

Later, Timur himself made use of elephants before the Mamluks near Aleppo (1400), took Damascus (1401) and Baghdad (1401), where he is said to have raised 120 pyramids, each one of 750 heads, making a total of 90,000 heads.

In 1402, he out-maneuvered the Ottoman ruler Bayazid—nicknamed "the Thunderbolt"—who arrived before Ankara with troops exhausted by several days' marching. The wells had been poisoned and the Ottomans had hardly any reserves of water left. A single day decided Bayazid's fate. By crushing the Ottomans, Timur unknowingly extended by half a century the life of Constantinople to which Bayazid had been laying siege on the eve of the conflict.

During the quarter of a century when he waged war in all directions, Timur had conquered, one after another, the Mongols of the

Golden Horde, the Mamluks, the janissaries, and other Ottoman troops—that is the best armies of the time. There remained China which death prevented him from invading: he died on the way there.

But the Timurids (1405-1507), unlike the Genghiskhanids, failed to retain the empire. Timur was the founder of an empire that disappeared shortly after his death. Twenty years after his departure, his grandson Ulugh Beg was defeated by the Uzbeks (1427). It is true that the Timurids retained power longer in Transoxiana and Khorasan, but by 1469 their domain had narrowed and been divided among various branches of the dynasty. Much of it fell into the hands of a Turkish-speaking group, the "White Horde" (*Ak Koyunlu*).

Following the classic pattern of his age and in accordance with his own tradition, Timur used terror to punish a city that refused to yield to his demands. Surrender at the first demand would ensure that lives were spared. Terror was used to dissuade other cities from holding out. That did not prevent numerous cities from refusing to surrender, thinking they would escape being sacked and destroyed: Baghdad, Ispahan, Saray, Astrakhan, etc. The usual practice was to build pyramids of heads that had been cut off. The *Zafer Nameh*, compiled under the patronage of one of Timur's grandsons and intended to exalt the memory of the conqueror, records these exactions with no attempt to minimize their extent, indeed quite the reverse. The perceptions of the time were different, at least among the victors. For military history, the anomaly is not in the self-satisfaction with which the victors of those days inflated the losses of the adversary, but, for example, in the innovation in history represented by the Western refusal to announce an estimate of the losses of Iraqi soldiers in the Gulf War in 1991.

But Timur, as was customary, spared the sherifs (presumed descendants of the Prophet), doctors of the law, famous philosophers and writers, engineers and architects as well as skilled artisans. Many of these were sent to Samarqand to embellish the conqueror's capital. Timur was concerned with culture and brought scholars and creative artists together in Samarqand where he protected them. He ordered the construction of architectural masterpieces that testify to his taste: the Bibi Khanum mosque, the Gur Emir, the Shah Zindeh.

It was the Uzbeks who, in the end, had the better of the Timurids.

The last Timurid to have left a mark on history, Babur (1483-1530), had a particularly eventful life. Although claiming to be a descendant of both Genghis and Timur, he was driven out of

Samarqand by the Uzbeks (1513) and failed to get back there despite his efforts. He ruled at Kabul, and, at the age of forty-two, decided to conquer India, at the head of some twelve thousand men. He met the forces of the Muslim sultanate near Delhi, in the plain of Panipat, and his artillery scattered the adversary's elephants (1526). He was the founder of the Mughal dynasty and left memoirs written in Chagatai.

The Rise of the Ottomans

It is well known that the rising power that had militarily overwhelmed Timur not far from Ankara in 1402, the Ottomans, had very modest origins. Fleeing the Mongols (1221), a Turkic tribe led by Ertoghrul, offered its services to the Seljukid sultan of Konya who granted him a fief not far from Constantinople. Ertohghrul's son embraced Islam and took the name of Osman (1291-1326). He founded the Ottoman (Osmanli) dynasty. It is perhaps pertinent to suggest that the later spread of Ottoman rule was one of the by-products of the Mongol conquest. That conquest and the terror it inspired drove various nomad groups (Turkomans, etc.) into Anatolia where they increased the proportion of Turkish-speakers.

The frontier culture that developed in Anatolia was dominated by the concept of holy war, while nomad traditions, especially in matters of warfare, continued to survive. There were endless tribal disputes among the various Turkish-speaking principalities while religiously inspired war took, or would soon take, three directions: to the west, the Byzantine empire or what remained of it; to the north, the Black Sea, also held by the Greeks; and to the south-east, Lesser Armenia.

Osman made himself master of Iznik and Brusa, and his successor, Orkhan, took Gallipoli (1354) and Adrianople (1361). This last city became the headquarters of the Ottoman principality.

The bases of the future empire were laid by Murad I (1362-1389), the conqueror of the Balkans. After 1365, the Byzantine empire, apart from a few minor possessions, was reduced to a small piece of land around Constantinople and its ramparts. The pope called for a crusade. Only the duke of Savoy came to help, retook Gallipoli (1366) and soon handed it over to the Byzantines.

While the Byzantine emperor himself went to Rome to beg for the pope's help, the Serbian princes were defeated at the battle of Maritza (1371). Gallipoli was retaken in 1379. But in the Balkans nothing was yet decided. And then Murad I had to return to Anatolia. In Konya, the Karamanids, who felt that they were the heirs of the Seljukids (of the sultanate of Rum), were defying the Ottomans. Murad finally defeated them in 1387. The Ottomans' adversaries were not all in the west. It took a further half century for the embryonic empire that Murad was endeavoring to build to be able to make a real claim to regional hegemony.

While Murad was defeating the Karamanids, the Balkans rebelled and he had to rush there. He defeated the Bulgars in 1387 and above all the kingdom of Serbia, at Kosovo, in 1389. Murad paid for that victory with his life.

Murad I created the corps of janissaries, which is reminiscent of the corps of gulhams, the military slaves that the Samanids had used several centuries earlier. It was a corps created by the forced draft (*devishirme*) of non-Muslim children, especially in the Balkans, made into Muslims, trained and broken to barrack life from their earliest years and forming an elite corps of infantry devoted to the reigning sultan.

No one was admitted among the janissaries except those recruited by the devishirme system. The janissaries' military code, especially when the institution was first founded, was strict, but later the corps intervened frequently in the succession. The code required

- Absolute obedience to officers. Complete submission to those in power.

- Not to practice any trade apart from that of arms and to be constantly improving in that.

- To refrain from all luxury unworthy of a soldier.

- Not to marry (this rule was later suppressed).

The corps of janissaries initially numbered five thousand, but, in the course of Ottoman history, that number was doubled, even trebled. The janissaries' reputation for invincibility came both from their excellence and their esprit de corps (strengthened by frequent homosexuality, which is not uncommon among elite troops in the history of many military societies[7]).

Murad I's successor, Bayazid ("the Thunderbolt") (Yildirim), proved to be particularly energetic. After having his brother executed (he might have pretended to the throne), he rushed to Anatolia to put down the principalities that had risen in revolt on the announcement of the death of Murad I. Taking advantage of the fact that he was occupied in bringing western Anatolia to heel, the Byzantines retook Gallipoli and the Vlachs crossed to the south of the Danube. Bayazid went over to the Balkans, drove the Vlachs back, and reconquered Salonika (1394).

To block the Ottomans, Sigismund, king of Hungary, appealed to the king of France. He sent some fourteen thousand horsemen under the command of the count of Nevers (the future John the Fearless, duke of Burgundy), who were joined on the way by a number of Englishmen, Germans, Swiss, and Poles. In 1396, at Nicopolis, this cavalry, which was only familiar with the frontal charge, initially broke through the Ottoman center but was caught in a pincer movement and massacred by the janissaries, while the Vlach, Transylvanian, and Hungarian auxiliaries on the wings fell back.

This victory enhanced Bayazid's reputation. The Ottomans were confirmed as a formidable military power. The following year, they subdued the Karamanids in Anatolia. Then they successfully attacked the sultan of Sivas. Siege was laid to Constantinople. Emperor Manuel II went to Rome to seek the help of a new crusade. However, just as Bayazid seemed destined to win the day, he was totally defeated by Timur not far from Ankara (1402).

The Ottoman war-machine—leaving aside the Hungarians—outclassed the armies of the peoples of the Balkans and the Danube basin, as well as the troops of the Turkish-speaking principalities of western Anatolia, but it was not up to facing Timur. He had triumphed over both the Golden Horde and the Mamluks.

The edifice was as yet still fragile. For Timur, Bayazid was nothing more than a bey, while Bayazid had sought the title of "sultan of Rum" from the Mamluks of Egypt in order to become the legitimate heir of the Seljukids of Anatolia.

But after Timur's victory, Bayazid's successors had to start all over again. The Hungarians continued to be influential in the Balkans and constituted a formidable power. The principalities of Anatolia, only recently reduced, were ready to revolt, especially as the possessions so hard won by Bayazid were now divided into three by brothers who were soon fighting one another. The Ottomans' center of gravity remained the Balkans, south of the Danube, with Adrianople as capital.

Following the death of Bayazid (1402), the interregnum was difficult. There were dynastic disputes that were eventually settled by a sultan, Mehmed, who had to be conciliatory towards the Turkish-speaking principalities of western Anatolia and not provoke conflict with Timur's successor, Shah Rukh.

After him, Murad II (1421-1451) also pursued a prudent policy. He was proclaimed sultan at Brusa and had at once to deal with the fact that Adrianople was in the hands of his uncle Mustapha who was defying his authority, and was, in fact, being backed by the Byzantines.

Murad succeeded in getting rid of his uncle and, in reprisal, laid siege to Constantinople for almost two months in 1422. But he had to go back to Anatolia, as the beys of Anatolia were not recognizing his authority. The Karamanids and the princes of Germiyan were supporting his younger brother, whom they proclaimed sultan. Murad was able to have his brother executed and defeat the beys of Kastamonu. But he was unable to subdue the Karamanids, who were protected by Timur's son, Shah Rukh.

For the seven years that followed 1423, Murad was chiefly concerned with waging a naval war against Venice whose fleet was much superior to his. In 1430, he retook Salonika, which had been ceded to Venice by Constantinople.

During this time, the kingdom of Hungary was pushing into Wallachia and Serbia. Murad was able to reoccupy Serbia but, in 1440, failed to take Belgrade, which was held by the Hungarians. The Hungarian counter-attack developed and in 1441-1442, the Ottomans were in extremely dire straits. Jan Hunyadi, at the head of Hungarian troops, inflicted defeat after defeat on the Ottomans. He retook Nish and Sofia and moved towards Constantinople. But peace was signed at Zlatica in 1443.

Murad now pursued a conciliatory policy. He withdrew from Serbia, whose ruler, George Brankovic, continued however to be one of his clients. He made peace with the Karamanids. In fact, in 1443, the Ottoman possessions in the Balkans were, in terms of size, rather small. Murad abdicated in favor of his son. It seemed a prudent moment to launch a crusade. It turned out to be only an expedition led by the Hungarians with Vlach soldiers and a considerable number of Western knights.

One last time, Westerners sought—without putting in the necessary resources—to loosen the vice around Constantinople. Murad II came out of retirement and resumed command of the army. The Serbs, led by George Brankovic, chose to stay neutral.

On 10 November 1444, the Western (chiefly Hungarian) cavalry was defeated at Varna, as it had been at Nicopolis. But Jan Hunyadi, nevertheless, was able to make three more murderous incursions against the Ottomans and endeavored to form an alliance with the Albanian insurgent Scanderbeg, who had been holding out against the Ottomans for almost two decades. Hunyadi was finally defeated at Kosovo in 1448.

Henceforth, the Balkans would remain under Ottoman control. Their tenacity had proved to be worthwhile. There remained Albania (1486) and the Peloponnese (1499). But the policy of prudence was not yet abandoned. Led by the grand vizier Chanderli, a policy was pursued of avoiding excessively overt domination in order to mollify the Anatolian principalities and the Christian princes in the Balkans.

That policy came to an end on the death of Murad II in 1451 and the victory in the palace of the most aggressive pashas. The young sultan Mehmed II was nineteen years old. Every new reign needed a military victory to secure itself. The decision was taken to lay siege to Constantinople and take it before the West could react.

The remarkable war-machine built up from the time of Murad I in the second half of the fourteenth century, with varying success, had succeeded in the space of a century in exercising its at least indirect control over western and central Anatolia and the Balkans south of the Danube, strangling Constantinople whose survival now depended only on its walls and possible maritime help from Genoa.

After a siege lasting fifty-four days, the Ottoman artillery overcame Constantinople, defended by some eight to ten thousand men, including a contingent of Genoese. The emperor died fighting.

At once, the territorial conquests of the Ottomans, which, until then, had been regarded by Timur or the Timurids or the Mamluks as the expansion of what they saw as a second-rank power, were transformed into a real imperial undertaking.

Moreover, very quickly, the fact of having finally succeeded after so many decades spent encircling the city led the Ottoman sultans to seek to build a universal empire, as it were to reanimate the Byzantine empire and its prestige under their auspices.

But first, Mehmed fought to re-establish his hegemony over the Balkans: the Morea was in the hands of the Venetians; the Serbian principality remained subject to Hungarian influence. Mehmed II failed to take Belgrade, which was held by the Hungarians (1456). But, in 1459,

Serbia finally fell into the hands of the Ottomans and this time was annexed. The following year, the Morea was occupied.

But there was a long war with Venice (1463-1471) and the naval superiority of the city of the Doges easily kept the Ottomans at bay. Venice sought an ally in the Ottomans' rear by concluding an alliance with the Ak Koyunlu of eastern Anatolia and Persia. Its fleet came right into the Dardanelles to beard Mehmed II.

Mehmed waged a campaign in Albania (1466-1467) to deal with Scanderberg once and for all, so that Ottoman domination south of the Danube should be complete.

Following in Timur's footsteps, Uzun Hasan, the ruler of the Ak Koyunlu who was master of Persia, intervened in central Anatolia. The Ottomans and the Karamanids were locked in conflict and the latter sought the help of Uzun Hasan. In 1472, an alliance was made embracing Venice, Cyprus, the Knights of Rhodes, and Uzun Hasan. His armies penetrated as far as Aksheir (1472), but the following year Mehmed halted Uzun Hasan's advance and he sued for peace. A year later, the Karamanids were vanquished.

The Ottomans and the Mamluks remained the two major Muslim powers in the eastern Mediterranean. The Mamluks had supported the Karamanids, arousing the Ottoman's hostility, but they refrained from challenging them.

Anatolia was at last subject to the Ottomans all the way to the Euphrates (1470). A few years later, in 1475, the khanate of the Crimea became a vassal state. The Ottomans now turned against Venice and managed to gain a foothold at Otranto in 1480, but failed to take Rhodes the same year. Mehmed died in 1481. In thirty years he had given the empire a firm base not only in central and western Anatolia but also in the Balkans as far as the Danube. Under Mehmed, the number of janissaries rose from five thousand to ten thousand men and they served as both the spearhead of the Ottoman army and the bastion of the ruling sultan. The power of the beys on the frontiers was reduced to the benefit of the central government. The grand vizier, appointed by the sultan, could not give orders to the janissaries. In the last resort, the sultan remained master in everything, and more particularly of the army and in the issuing of laws (*qanun-name*). The problem of the succession continued to be a crucial issue all though Ottoman history. Mehmed's *qanun-name* decreed that on accession to the throne the successor's brothers might be killed. On the death of Mehmed II, a revolt by the janissaries broke out as two claimants disputed the throne. One of them, Bayazid (1481-1512), was brought to power. He was infinitely less powerful than his predecessor. The notables, kept in check by Mehmed, wanted more power. Bayazid clashed with the Mamluks who felt they were superior to the Ottomans because they held the caliphate. Hostilities (1485-1491) ended in deadlock.

The war with Venice (1499-1502) showed that Venetian naval power was greater than that of the Ottomans.

The most serious danger hanging over Ottoman power at the beginning of the sixteenth century came from Persia. Shah Ismaël, who was Shiite, played on the "red heads" (*qizil bash*) of Anatolia.

Bayazid's reign stands out as a period of respite from conquest, which came to an end with the coming to power of Selim Yavuz, known as the Cruel (1512-1520).

He was an energetic conqueror; he began by eliminating every member of the dynasty who might have laid claim to the throne. He sought to engage in peaceful relations with Hungary in order to have a free hand in the east, against the Safavids. He engaged in the mass execution of supporters of shah Ismaël in eastern Anatolia and, in the name of Sunnism, attacked the shah, who was defeated at Chaldiran in 1514. But the conflict with Persia continued for over a century.

Dyarbakir was taken the following year. Two years later, the Mamluks were defeated in Syria. Until then, the Ottomans had been a power astride western Anatolia and the Balkans south of the Danube, but now as the sixteenth century began, it became a Middle Eastern power, and thus became caught up in the politics of the Arab Muslim world.

In 1517, Egypt was conquered and Mamluk rule came to an end. From then on, the caliphate was exercised from Istanbul.

The Ottoman empire was now fully an empire, and the sultan was the most powerful ruler of Islam and the protector of the religion— and of its holy places: Mecca and Medina. The area of the empire at this time equaled that of the Byzantine empire on the eve of Muslim expansion.

With Suleyman, the empire reached its zenith. Victory followed victory: he took Belgrade (1521) and Rhodes (1522) and above all won the victory of Mohacz against the Hungarians (1526) and laid siege to Vienna (1529). Before long Suleyman was caught up in the rivalry between Francis I and the Hapsburgs. In the east, he took Baghdad in 1534, and in the Mediterranean, Rhodes in 1570.

At the same time, the Ottomans successfully endeavored to establish their domination in the Mediterranean. The fleets of the Holy League under the Genoese admiral Andrea Doria were defeated at Preveza (on the western coast of Greece) in 1538. Control of the Mediterranean almost passed into the hands of the Ottomans. Malta and the Knights who held the fortress were able to hold out against them (1565) and were relieved by Spanish intervention.

A halt was exercised at the battle of Lepanto in 1571 by the fleet of the Holy League (Spain, Venice, Papal States). Two years later, the Russians stopped the Ottomans before Astrakhan. Not long after, in 1586, shah Abbas of Persia launched a counter-attack.

Yet, although it had almost reached its maximum extent on virtually every front, the Ottoman empire remained an extremely formidable power. Until the formation of the army of Louis XIV it was without any doubt the greatest military power in both Europe and the Orient. Military decline came only at the end of the seventeenth century, at the time of the treaty of Carlowitz, when the empire began its gradual and inexorable retreat.

Montecuccoli, one of the great generals of the seventeenth century, who, fighting in the service of the Hapsburgs, defeated the Ottoman forces at the battle of Saint Gotthard in 1662, observed that, in dealing with Ottoman troops, one had to be careful of two things: not to let oneself be enveloped by the wings while the adversary allows you to advance in the center, and not to be tempted to pursue the enemy who, most often, feigns flight so as to take advantage of the pursuers' disordered advance. These, like harassment, were techniques inherited from the steppe and still very much alive, as the Crusaders had encountered them on the Anatolian front in the twelfth century, without knowing their origin.

It was in the Ottoman empire that Genghis Khan's ideal of world domination was reborn. The Ottoman empire, unlike all other Muslim states, was based on a dynastic principle foreign to Islam: unshakeable loyalty to the family of Osman.... That loyalism is reminiscent of that of the Turkic-Mongol tribes for the family of Genghis.[8]

The Eyewitnesses

The Coming of the Mongols

"These were a people who emerged from the confines of China, and attacked the cities of Turkestan, like Kashgar and Balasaghun, and thence advanced on the cities of Transoxiana, such as Samarqand, Bukhara, and the like, taking possession of them, and treating their inhabitants in such wise as we shall mention; and of them one division then passed on into Khurasan, until they had made an end of taking possession, and destroying, and slaying, and plundering, and thence passing on to Ray, Haematein and the Highlands, and the cities contained therein, even to the limits of Iraq, whence they marched on the towns of Adharbayjan and Arraniyya, destroying them and slaying most of their inhabitants, of whom none escaped save a small remnant; and all this in less than a year; this is a thing whereof the like hath not been heard. And when they had finished with Adharbayjan and Arraniyya, they passed on to Darband-i-Shirwan, and occupied its cities, none of which escaped save the fortress wherein was their King; wherefore they passed by it to the countries of the Lan and the Lakiz, and the various nationalities which dwell in that region, and plundered, slew, and destroyed them to the full. And thence they made their way to the lands of Qipchaq, who are the most numerous of the Turks, and slew all such as withstood them, while the survivors fled to the fords and mountain-tops, and abandoned their country, which these Tartars overran. All this they did in the briefest space of time, remaining only for so long as their march required and no more.

Another division, distinct from that mentioned above, marched on Ghazna and its dependencies, and those parts of India, Sistan and Kirman which border thereon, and wrought therein deeds like unto the other, nay, yet more grievous. Now this is a thing the like of which ear hath not heard; for Alexander, concerning whom historians agree that he conquered the world, did not do so with such swiftness, but only in the space of about ten years; neither did he slay, but was satisfied that men should be subject to him. But these Tartars conquered most of the habitable globe, and the best, the most flourishing and most populous part thereof, and that whereof the inhabitants were the most advanced in character and conduct, in about a year; nor did any country escape their devastations which did not fearfully expect them and dread their arrival.

Moreover they need no commissariat, nor the conveyance of supplies, for they have with them sheep, cows, horses, and the like quadrupeds, the flesh of which they eat, [needing] naught else. As for their beasts which they ride, these dig into the earth with their hoofs and eat the roots of plants, knowing naught of barley. And so, when they alight anywhere, they have need of nothing from without."[9]

Of Merv and the Fate Thereof

"On the next day, which was the first of Muharram 618 [25th of February 1221], and the last of the lives of most of the inhabitants of Merv, Toli, that furious lion, arrived with an army like unto a dark night and a raging sea and in multitude exceeding the sands of the desert...

He advanced in person to the Gate of Victory together with some five hundred horses and rode right round the town; and for six days they inspected the outworks, walls, moat... and reached the conclusion that the townspeople's supplies would suffice to defend them and that the walls were a stout bastion that would withstand their attack.

On the seventh day,...the armies gathered together and halted before the Shahristan Gate. They joined battle, some two hundred men issuing from the gate and attacking. Toli dismounted in person...and advanced upon them. And the Mongols attacked in his company driving them back into the town. Others issued forth from another gate but the Mongols stationed there repelled the attack. And so the townspeople were nowhere able to achieve any result and could not even put their heads out of the gates. Finally,...the Mongols took up positions in several rings around the fortifications and kept watch throughout the night, so that none had any means of egress.

Mujir-al-Mulk saw no way out save surrender and submission. In the morning, therefore,...he dispatched Jamal-ad-Din, one of the chief *imams* of Merv, as his ambassador and sued for quarter. Being reassured by fair words and promises, he got together presents from the quadrupeds in the town—horses, camels and mules—and went to Toli [in person]. Toli questioned him about the town and asked for details about the wealthy and notable...

The Mongols now entered the town and drove all the inhabitants, nobles and commoners, out on to the plain. For four days and nights the people continued to come out of the town; the Mongols detained them all, separating the women from the men. Alas! how many [fairy-faced] ones did they drag from the bosoms of their husbands! How many sisters did they separate from their brothers! How many parents were distraught at the ravishment of their virgin daughters!

The Mongols ordered that, apart from four hundred artisans whom they specified and selected from amongst the men and some children, girls and boys, whom they bore off into captivity, the whole population, including the women and children, should be killed, and no one, whether woman or man, be spared. The people of Merv were then distributed among the soldiers and levies, and, in short, to each man was allotted the execution of three or four hundred persons."[10]

The Mongols in Armenia

"One could see swords mercilessly cutting down men and women, youths and children, old men and old women, bishops, priests, deacons, and clerks. Suckling children were hurled against the rocks, beautiful virgins were raped and enslaved.

It was frightful to behold their appearance and their cruel lack of compassion; they pitied not a single mother's tears nor a single grey head, but went on punishing and killing as if enjoying themselves at a wedding or a drinking-bout.

The whole country filled up with the corpses of the dead yet there was no one to bury them. Tears appeared in the eyes of lovers but no one dared to weep, out of fear of the impious ones.

The country was draped in mourning and its magnificent beauty was destroyed. Its worship was blocked and mass ceased to be offered at its altars, the singing of songs was no longer heard. The whole land was plunged into darkness and people preferred the night to the day. The country was drained of its inhabitants and foreigners moved about in it.

Goods and property were ravished, though their greedy nature could never be satisfied. Houses and rooms were searched and there was nothing left that they did not take. They moved about here and there like swift mountain goats and wrecked and tore things apart like wolves. Their horses did not tire at the pace, nor did [the Mongols] tire of amassing booty.

Thus severity was visited upon many peoples and tongues for the cup of the Lord's wrath poured down over the country in vengeance for our wicked deeds and for sinning before Him; and His just rage was kindled. Therefore the entrance [of the Mongols] into every land was made easy. As soon as they had captured all lands, they gathered up all the animals (those which had fled and those which had not), the goods and property and multitude of slaves, which were out in open areas.

Thereafter they battled with all the fortresses and with many cities, erecting diverse types of [siege] machinery, for they were clever and capable. They took and tore down many fortresses and keeps. It was summertime and extremely hot, and provisions had not been gathered in, for [the Mongols] came upon them unexpectedly. Therefore men and beasts suffered from thirst and, willingly or unwillingly fell into the hands of the enemy because of the danger facing them. And there were those they killed, and those they kept as slaves for their needs. They treated similarly the densely populated cities, encamping about them and besieging them."[11]

The Battle of the River Kalka (1224)

"That year, for our sins, unknown tribes came. No one knew who they were nor whence they came nor what their faith nor what their language, and some called them Tartars...

We learned that they had conquered many countries and killed many people...

Only one Russian warrior in ten escaped death during that battle. And as they returned home, many of those that did survive were killed by the Polovtsis...

As for the Tartars, they returned to the other side of the Dniepr and we know not whence they came, nor whither they went...

God alone knows who sent them for our sins."[12]

The Story of the Destruction of Riazan (1242)

"And Batu, the accursed, began the conquest of the land of Riazan, and before long got near the city itself.

They encircled the cities and fought without let for five days. Batu frequently rotated his troops with fresh ones while the inhabitants of Riazan fought without respite. And many inhabitants were killed and others wounded. Others again were exhausted with fatigue or from their wounds.

On the dawn of the sixth day, the infidel warriors began to invest the city.... And they seized the city of Riazan on 21 December [1243]. And the Tartars entered the Cathedral of the Assumption of the Blessed Virgin and they shattered in pieces the princess Agrippina, her daughters-in-law and the other princesses. They burned the bishops and the priests and set fire to the church. And they massacred countless people, including women and children. Others were drowned in the river.... And they burned this holy city with all its glories and its riches and they captured the kin of the princes of Riazan, the princes of Kiev and Chernigov. And the churches of

God were destroyed and much blood was shed upon the holy altars. And no one was left alive. All were dead. All had drunk the same bitter cup to the full.... And no one was left to keep vigil over the dead. Fathers and mothers could not keep vigil over their dead children, nor could the children keep vigil over their fathers and mothers.... All were dead. And all this happened for our sins...

There was a city of Riazan in the land of Riazan but its glory is no more and nothing remains to be seen in the city except smoke, ashes and bare earth. All the churches and the cathedral were abandoned to the flames. And not only this city but many others were conquered. The sound of bells and the sound of the offices are heard no more. And instead of joy there is now nothing but lamentations without end."[13]

Beliefs and Customs of the Mongols

"Whenever possible they ate and drank insatiably, but when it was not possible, they were temperate.... When eating, lords and servants share equally...

They take as many women as they want but they do not let prostitutes live among their women. However, wherever they chance upon foreign women, they copulate with them indiscriminately. [The Mongols] loathe theft so much that they torture to death anyone caught at it.

There is no religion or worship among them, but they frequently call on the name of God in all matters. We do not know (nor do they) if this is to thank the God of Being or some other thing that they call god. However, usually they say that their king is a relative of God. God took heaven as his portion and gave earth to the Khan, for they say that Chingiz-Khan, the father of the [present] Khan was not born from the seed of man but that a light came from the unseen, entered through a skylight in the home, and announced to his mother: 'Conceive and you will bear a son who will be ruler of the world.' And they say that [Chingiz-Khan] was born from that."[14]

Of Discipline among the Mongols

"For they have divided all the people into companies of ten, appointing one of the ten to be the commander of the nine others; while from among each ten commanders one has been given the title of 'commander of the hundred,' all the hundred having been placed under his command. And so it is with each thousand men and so also with each ten thousand, over whom they have appointed a commander whom they call 'commander of the *tümen* [ten thousand].' In accordance with this arrangement, if in an emergency any man or thing be required, they apply to the commanders of *tümen*; who in turn apply to the commanders of thousands, and so on down to the commanders of tens. There is true equality in this; each man toils as much as the next, and no difference is made between them, no attention being paid to wealth or power. If there is a sudden call for soldiers an order is issued that so many thousand men must present themselves in such and such a place at such and such an hour of that day or night. 'They shall not retard it [their appointed time] an hour; and they shall not advance it.'[15] And they arrive not a twinkling of an eye before or after the appointed hour. Their obedience and submissiveness is such that if there be a commander of a hundred thousand between whom and the Khan there is a distance of sunrise and sunset, and if he but commit some fault, the Khan dispatches a single horseman to punish him after the manner prescribed: if his head has been demanded, he cuts if off, and if gold be required, he takes it from him...

Another *yasa* [law] is that no man may depart to another unit than the hundred, thousand or ten to which he has been assigned, nor may he seek refuge elsewhere. And if this order be transgressed the man who transferred is executed in the presence of the troops, while he that received him is severely punished."[16]

The Postal System (Yam) of the Mongols

"Again, when the extent of their territories became broad and vast and important events fell out, it became essential to ascertain the activities of their enemies, and it was also necessary to transport goods from the West to the East and from the Far East to the West. Therefore throughout the length and breadth of the land they established *yams* [post stations], and made arrangements for the upkeep and expenses of each *yam*, assigning thereto a fixed number of men and beasts as well as food, drink and other necessities. All this they shared out among the *tümen*, each two *tümen* having to supply one *yam*. Thus, in accordance with the census, they so distribute and exact the charge, that messengers need make no long detour in order to obtain fresh mounts while at the same time the peasantry and the army are not placed in constant inconvenience. Moreover strict orders were issued to the messengers with regard to the sparing of the mounts, etc., to recount all of which would delay us too long.

Every year the *yams* are inspected, and whatever is missing or lost has to be replaced by the peasantry."[17]

How to Fight Mongols

"The army should be organised in the same way as the Tartar army, under captains of a thousand, captains of a hundred, captains of ten and the chiefs of the army. The last named ought on no account to take part in the battle, just as the Tartar chiefs take no part, but they should watch the army and direct it. They should make a law that all advance together either to battle or elsewhere in order appointed. Severe punishment ought to be meted out to anyone who deserts another either going into battle or fighting, or takes flight when they are not retreating as a body, for if this happens a section of the Tartar force follows those fleeing and kills them with arrows while the rest fight those who have remained on the field, and so both those who stay and those who run away are thrown into confusion and killed. Similarly anyone who turns aside to take plunder before the army of the enemy has been completely vanquished ought to be punished with a very heavy sentence; among the Tartars such a one is put to death without any mercy. The chiefs of the army should choose their battle ground, if possible a flat plain, every part of which they can watch, and if they can they should have a large forest behind them or on their flank, so situated however that the Tartars cannot come between them and the wood. The army ought not to assemble into one body, but many lines should be formed, separated from each other, only not too far apart. One line ought to be sent to meet the first line of the Tartars to approach; if the Tartars feign flight they ought not to pursue them very far, certainly not further than they can see, in case the Tartars lead them into ambushes they have prepared, which is what they usually do. And let another line be in readiness to help the first if occasion require it.

Moreover they ought to have scouts in every direction, before, to the right and to the left, to see when the other lines of Tartars are coming, and one line ought always to be sent to meet each Tartar line, for the Tartars always strive to surround their enemies; the greatest precautions ought to be taken to prevent their doing this, for in this way an army is easily vanquished."[18]

Ibn Khaldun was in Damascus when Timur laid siege to it. He was one of the leading figures sent in an embassy to negotiate. He relates his meeting with the conqueror in his autobiography:

He then summoned the emirs of his government who were in charge of building matters; they brought in the foremen of construction, the engineers, and discussed whether by leading off the water which flows round the moat of the Citadel they could by this operation discover its ingress. They discussed this for a long time in his council, then left...

Then he pressed the siege of the Citadel in earnest; he erected against it catapults, naphtha guns, ballistas, and breachers, and within a few days sixty catapults and other similar engines were set up. The siege pressed ever harder upon those within the Citadel, and its structure was destroyed on all sides. Therefore the men [defending it], among them a number of those who had been in the service of the Sultan, and those whom he had left behind, asked for peace. Timur granted them amnesty, and after they were brought before him the Citadel was destroyed and its vestiges completely effaced.

From the inhabitants of the town he confiscated under torture hundredweights of money which he seized having taken all the property, mounts, and tents which the ruler of Egypt had left behind. Then he gave permission for the plunder of the houses of the people of the city, and they were despoiled of all their furniture and goods. The furnishings and utensils of no value which remained were set on fire, and the fire spread to the walls of the houses, which were supported on timbers. It continued to burn until it reached the Great Mosque; the flames mounted to its roof, melting the lead in it, and the ceilings and walls collapsed. This was an absolutely dastardly and abominable deed, but the changes in affairs are in the hands of Allah—he does with his creatures as he wishes, and decides in his kingdom as he wills..."[19]

Notes

1.   P. Ratchnevsky, *Genghis Khan, His Life and Legacy*, trans. T. N. Haining (Oxford: Blackwell, 1991).
2.   Not to be confused with the precepts or *biligs* of Genghis Khan. "Man's greatest good fortune is to chase and defeat his enemy, seize his total possessions, leave his married women weeping and wailing, ride his gelding, use the bodies of his women as a nightshirt and support, gazing upon and kissing their rosy breasts, sucking their lips which are sweet as the berries of their breasts." Rashideddin, *Djami at-Tawarikh*, as quoted in Ratchnevsky, op. cit., 153).
3.   See Basil Liddell Hart, *Great Captains Unveiled* (London, 1927).
4.   "*'Mein Gott'*, said a Croat Captain, who dined with me in 1815, 'a man can eat well without all these trimmings. When we are in the field and feel hungry, we shoot down the first animal that comes our way, cut off a good hunk of flesh, salt it a little,... and put it under our saddle...; then we gallop for a while after which...we feed like princes." J.-A. Brillat-Savarin, *La Physiologie du goût* (Paris: Flammarion, "Champs") (first pub. 1825), trans. A. Dayton, *The Philosopher in the Kitchen* (Harmondsworth: Penguin Books, 1970).
5.   Under Kilawan, a remarkable organizer of the Mamluk army (1279-1290), the army took the last Crusader fortresses. Al Malik an Nasr (1293-1341) repulsed the Mongols in 1299-1301. In 1375, the Mamluks pursued their advance northward and destroyed the Armenian kingdom of Cilicia.
6.   But one is quite amazed to find an expert on the Turks making assertions such as: "As for the law on toleration, which, more than the others, was one of the key features of the empire, it is not obvious that it was included in the 'Yasaq'. No law

ordains what is self-evident. Man does not have to be forced to eat, drink or sleep. There is every reason to believe that a Mongol had no need to be told to respect the opinions of others. It was a need as innate as the need to breathe." J.-P. Roux, *Histoire des Mongols* (Paris: Fayard, 1993), 145.

7.   Ancient Greece, Japan, etc.
8.   Chantal Lemercier-Quelquejay, *La Paix mongole* (Paris: Flammarion, 1963).
9.   Ibn al-Athir (1160-1223), *Complete History*, in *A Literary History of Persia*, ed. E. G. Browne (Cambridge: Cambridge University Press, 1902).
10.   Juvaini, *History of the World Conqueror* in *The Islâmic World*, ed. W. H. McNeil and M. Robinson Waldman (New York: Oxford University Press, 1973).
11.   Kirakos Gandzakets'i, *History of the Armenians*, trans. Robert Bedrosian (New York: Sources of the Armenian Tradition, 1986), 201-203.
12.   *Novgorod Chronicle,* anonymous, thirteenth century.
13.   In C. Lemercier-Quelquejay, *La Paix mongole*, op. cit.
14.   Kirakos Gandzakets'i, *History of the Armenians*, op. cit., 234-235.
15.   *Koran*, sura VII, verse 32.
16.   Juvaini, *History of the Conqueror of the World*, op. cit.
17.   Ibid.
18.   John of Plano Carpino, *History of the Mongols*, in *The Mongol Mission*, ed. C. Dawson (London: Sheed and Ward, 1955).
19.   In W. Fischel, *Ibn Khaldun and Tamerlane. Their Historic Meeting in Damascus, 1401 A.D. (803 A.H.)* (Berkeley: University of California Press, 1952).

4

The Revenge of the Sedentary Peoples (Sixteenth-Nineteenth Centuries)

The preeminence of nomads or their near heirs remained total until the fifteenth century and only came to an end in the mid-sixteenth century. From that time onward, the history of central Asia became, to all intents and purposes, local history. Only China, in the mid-seventeenth century, experienced total disaster due to the Manchus.

Elsewhere, the heirs of the sons of the steppe had already been ruling sedentary empires for several generations: the Ottomans had taken Constantinople in the mid-fifteenth century; Babur had conquered northern India in the first quarter of the sixteenth century.

Yet the nomads of High Asia continued to be formidable after the mid-sixteenth century, and remained so until the mid-eighteenth century.

The Oirat Mongol empires threatened China until 1758, when the Manchu dynasty, which had meanwhile become sinicized, resumed the traditional policy of China and put an end to their power. It was again the Manchu dynasty that took Sinkiang and restored to China an area of domination to the north-west even more extensive than that of the most aggressive Chinese dynasties (the Han and the T'ang).

But it was Russia that played the major role in the history of central Asia in the period from the sixteenth century to the end of the nineteenth century.

Russia after the Mongols

During the centuries of Mongol rule, the Russians became familiar with the tactics and fighting ethos of the Mongols. They equipped themselves with strip armor that was nomad in origin. At the end of the fourteenth century, under the leadership of Dmitri Donskoi who introduced general conscription, the Russians briefly overcame the Mongols. The Russian victory at the battle of Kulikovo (1380) was widely celebrated. But shortly after, in 1382, the Golden Horde, led by Tuqtamish, crushed the Russian forces and the Tartar yoke continued for another century.

From the beginning of the thirteenth century to the end of the fifteenth, the Golden Horde, although weakened after the middle of the fifteenth century, remained unbeaten apart from the setbacks inflicted by the great Timur. And even that was rather all in the family. The sole attempt to invade the territories held by the Mongols was made by the grand duke of Lithuania. It was a failure (1399). The Golden Horde weakened itself by splitting. First, the khanate of Kazan (1438) was established, then the khanate of the Crimea (1441) and, shortly after, the khanate of Astrakhan. The Golden Horde disappeared in 1502, brought down by its own divisions and the policy of Ivan III who allied with the khanate of the Crimea against the khanate of Kazan.

The initial impact of the Mongols in China was disastrous, but prosperity was restored with the reign of Khubilai. Transoxiana and western Iran recovered quite quickly. In eastern Iran (Khorasan), the damage was extremely serious, coming as it did on top of the harm done to Iranian agriculture by the coming of the Seljukids. That region never recovered its former prosperity. Russia took a long time to recover. Southern Ukraine had already suffered severely from the Pechenegs and the Kipchaks, and the passage of the Mongols dealt the country a deathblow. In the north, apart from a few cities that escaped, not tribute but direct rule, such as Novgorod and Pskov, craft-work disappeared, as did quasi-democratic urban institutions such as the *veche*. The Mongols imposed rule by the descendants of Rurik (the princes of Moscow) as the only legitimate one and thus contributed to the institution of tsarism. The *pax mongolica,* which prevailed for a century and a half in the thirteenth and fourteenth centuries, was dearly paid for by the defeated. Yet it did make possible contacts and trade between China and Europe through the Middle East. For the first time in a very long time, the Eurasian landmass communicated along the "silk roads": the northern route through Beijing, Karakorum, Otrar, Tana, and Caffa; and the southern route through Tarim, Kashgar, Khorassan, Kazvin, Tabriz, and then Trebizond or Cilicia.

But occupied Russia no longer communicated with Western Europe as it had done previously. It became "semi-Asiatic."

Ivan III proclaimed the end of the Tartar yoke in 1480, but in 1521 the khan of Kazan crushed the Russian army and laid siege to Moscow. It was only in 1552 that Ivan IV, known as "the Terrible," went on the counter-attack. With one hundred and fifty cannon, he took Kazan, and then Astrakhan (1557). The khanate of the Crimea was beyond his reach, and it remained a formidable power. In 1571, Moscow was taken and sacked yet again by the Tartars of the khanate of the Crimea. Ivan IV agreed to pay them a tribute, which the Russians continued paying until the reign of Peter the Great, at the beginning of the eighteenth century! While cannon could overcome cities with dilapidated fortifications or break a charge, they could not do much against harassment by the Tartar cavalry. The musket was very slow to recharge, and had a smaller range than the nomad's bow until the seventeenth century and was thus only moderately effective. A new Tartar incursion took place into the heart of Muscovy in 1591, but Moscow was never taken by the nomads again. However, a secure grip on the Kazan region, peopled by Tartars, Volga Bulgars, and Finns, was really achieved only in the mid-seventeenth century

Russian geopolitics led the initial expansion eastward. The advance of the Cossack Yermak, who had been condemned to death for rebellion and undertook the conquest of Siberia with a hundred and fifty companions to rehabilitate himself, began in 1581. Tobolsk was reached in 1587. The conquest was spread over some sixty years, the high points being the destruction of the khanate of Sibir in 1598 and reaching the Sea of Okhotsk in 1643.

Most of this rapid advance took place north of the steppes, in thinly populated areas. The drive to the Black Sea, however, was painfully slow. From the beginning of the seventeenth century, there was a hard-won advance towards the black lands. The peasants, pressured by both the state and the landlords, sometimes turned Cossack, thus escaping serfdom, and went to live free in border areas, facing the Tartar threat.

In the mid-sixteenth century, the Moscow government built a system of fortifications equipped with garrisons along the tributaries of the Oka and the Don. This colonization was very slow. The Crimean Tartars made annual incursions, and they simply had to be accepted as a fact of life. After 1591, they never again crossed the Oka, but under Peter the Great, there were still raids around Kharkov (1710-1718). The Crimea was a thousand kilometers south of the Oka, and, for two centuries, the Tartars seized women and children as well as men and sold them as slaves to the Ottoman empire at Caffa, on the Black Sea.

The Russians only gained control of Kiev in 1667, although Kazan had been under Russian rule since 1552 and Russia had access to the Pacific by 1643.

Until the late seventeenth century, the Russians were confined to the forest and tundra areas. They were fur traders. As they moved eastward, they met only two serious pockets of resistance, from the Buriats, near Lake Baikal, and from the Manchus, near the Amur River, before they encountered the Chinese empire.

As time went by, the lines of colonization protected by forts advanced southward. From the line along the Oka, in the sixteenth century, the Donetz was reached by about 1600. By 1650, five or six hundred kilometers more had been gained. But the Tartars remained formidable and they could field up to thirty thousand mounted men. In addition, the khanate of the Crimea allied now with the Poles, now with the Zaporizhian Cossacks against Russia. In 1633, the Russians reorganized the defense system and resumed their advance. *As was the case with the United States, it was an advance of farmers against nomads. Colonization was the most profound Russian experience after the Mongol occupation.* The Russians only moved from defense to offense when the frontier was well south of the wooded steppe. They succeeded with great difficulty in solving the problems of logistics in the vast spaces of the open steppe between the Donetz and the Crimea (1687), and it was only at the end of the seventeenth century that they were finally in a position to deal directly with territory of the Crimean Tartars who then had no choice but to use a scorched earth tactic. The khans ceded the fortress of Azov in 1699. In the same year, the peace of Carlowitz, signed with the Ottoman empire, meant that *for the first time in two centuries, the Black Sea ceased to be a Turkish lake.* Peter the Great secured lasting control of Azov in 1711. The Bashkir Tartars supported the protest movement headed by Stenka Razin (1667-1671) and the failure of the great revolt by Pugachev (1772-1774) brought down with it the Kazakhs of the "Little Horde" who had joined it.

The Russian people must have had unusual reserves of robustness, after two and a half centuries of direct or indirect Mongol yoke, to go on such a sustained counter-offensive. The Russians' achievement was less in the conquest of central Siberia by the Cossacks in less than a century (sixteenth-seventeenth centuries)—remarkable as that was—but in the tenacious conquest or reconquest of Ukraine and then the Crimea. It took centuries of unrelenting struggle to cover the distance that separated the Muscovy of the heirs of Ivan the Terrible from the Sea of Azov. There were lines of small forts held by Cossacks and small peasant populations, where deadly incursions by Crimean Tartars were an ever-present threat. The Tartars, with their backs against the Ottoman empire, held out until the last quarter of the eighteenth century. As the French revolution was breaking out, the Crimean Tartars had just been vanquished.

Catherine II's successes in her war with the Ottoman empire (1768-1774) sealed the fate of the khanate. The Crimea became Russian. After half a millennium (1240-1783), the last remnant of the heirs of Genghis Khan in Europe disappeared.

Russia demonstrated an extraordinary vitality both demographically and militarily in the southern lands gained at such cost in the seventeenth and eighteenth centuries. Then it set about the Kazakh lands (1770-1844); and did so before the great imperial drive of the era of European colonialism in the second half of the nineteenth century. No state, not even China, contributed so much to defeating, driving back, and subduing the great warrior nomads of a bygone age that had cost Russia so dear.

This colonizing step-by-step advance by the Russians, fought all the way, was possible not simply because of superior firepower (a dubious proposition in any event before the seventeenth century) but because of demography. The population of Russia, that is principally the Slavs, rose from 10 million in 1600 to 30 million in 1800 and 70 million in 1850. Russia's adversary to the south, the Ottoman empire, for example, which had 28 million inhabitants in 1600, had fewer than 25 million by 1700 and did not rise above that number until its fall. When the Tsarist empire reached its greatest territorial extent at the end of the nineteenth century, the proportion of Muslims and other peoples of nomad origin was under 10 percent.

The Russian advance, which had known no extended respite since the second half of the sixteenth century, became a rush in the second half of the nineteenth century. Unlike other European imperialisms, this colonization took place over contiguous territory. After securing the land inhabited by the Kazakhs, following a prolonged effort, the Russians seized the lands of the Uzbeks in twenty years: the khanates of Kokand, Bukhara, and Khiva fell between 1853 and 1873. Samarqand was taken in 1858 and the largest city in central Asia, Tashkent, in 1865. After securing the Uzbek khanates, the Russians attacked the land of the Turkmens whose conquest in the early 1880s proved very costly. Against the background of Russo-British and Russo-Chinese rivalry, the conquest of central Asia was completed with control of the Pamirs (1895).

Nominally, a descendant of Genghis Khan ruled over the khanate of Khiva until the establishment of Bolshevik power in the region in 1920.

China after the Mongols

The Mongol Yuan dynasty came to an end in 1368. The Ming (1368-1644) were an expression of national restoration. Until the end of the fifteenth century, the Ming conducted an offensive policy. It was these years that saw the seven expeditions led by admiral Cheng Ho (a Muslim eunuch from Yunnan), which stretched over the years 1403 to 1433 and took the Chinese fleet as far as the coast of east Africa. At that date, the Portuguese had not even reached Madeira. But in the second half of the fifteenth century, the threats reappeared and the Ming opted to enclose themselves. The Great Wall of China was repaired as pressure from the nomads made itself felt once again, while Japanese pirates constituted a threat from the sea. The coast was abandoned to these latter. The Oirots, who later came to be called Kalmyks, were the dominant power in western Mongolia in the mid-fifteenth century, and, led by a chief who successfully imposed his rule, Esen (1439-1455), invaded northern China. They captured the Ming emperor in 1450, but failed to take Beijing. The Ming built a wall to protect the weak point in their northern defense arrangements: the Ordos. This was completed in 1474. In fact, the Great Wall of China, as we know it today, was completed in 1540.

Meanwhile, in the second half of the fifteenth century, a new threat appeared with the eastern Mongols, the Khalkas (the Oirots came from western Mongolia). Under the command of Dayan Khan (1470-1543) who defeated Chinese troops in 1542, and his grandson Altan Khan (1543-1583), the nomads once again penetrated into China and threatened Beijing (1555). After that date, China lived enclosed in its declining power. Disputes within the dynasty itself at the end of the first half of the seventeenth century led one faction to seek help from the Manchus, whose power had been steadily growing under an outstanding leader, Nurachi. He proclaimed himself khan of the Chin (1616), thereby showing that he was linking up with a past when the ancestors of the Manchus (the Chin) had reigned over northern China. Two years later, he published a manifesto against the Ming. He died in 1626, but his son seized power when he was called on for help by one of the Ming parties. The Manchu dynasty reigned over China from 1644 to 1911, until the establishment of the republic.

In the course of the second half of the seventeenth century, the Khalkas submitted to the Manchus. But in the reign of Galdan Khan (1676-1697) a renaissance of nomad power occurred which historians of central Asia sometimes describe as the "second Oirot empire." With Galdan Khan, the Mongol nomads who dominated much of eastern-central Asia launched a series of massive raids against the Manchus, only to be defeated in 1696 by the cannon supplied by the Jesuits to the K'ang-Hsi emperor, but they remained formidable until their final destruction in 1758. During the eighteenth century, China annexed Sinkiang and began to encroach upon Kazakh lands.

***

The Manchu dynasty resumed the traditional geopolitics of conquering Chinese dynasties, triumphed over its nomad adversaries to the north and restored an imperial China that stretched westward to within just a few hundred kilometers of Talas, where the battle between the Muslims and the Chinese had occurred in 751, marking the maximum westward expansion of Chinese imperialism.

The Chinese colonization policy in the provinces of Sinkiang and Kansu precipitated a series of Muslim revolts in the nineteenth century (1818, 1834, 1855, 1862-1877, 1895).

From the mid-nineteenth century the Russians were on the Chinese empire, as a result of their territorial proximity. The first Russo-Chinese treaty dates from 1869. It was followed by other unequal treaties that deprived the Chinese empire of 2.5 million square kilometers of territory along the Ussouri and in the Pacific region. These areas were largely home to nomads.[1] The warrior nomads who had once caused the world to tremble were overwhelmed by the onslaughts of the Chinese and above all the Russians.

Epilogue

World geopolitics was long largely determined by the nomads of High Asia—which was the pivot of the Eurasian landmass—and by the nomads' heirs, once these had become Islamized. When Europe became really preponderant, classical geopolitics was articulated not on the opposition between nomads and sedentary peoples but on the opposition between sea powers and continental powers, the pivot continuing to be situated in the heart of central Asia, as the British Halford Mackinder suggested.

The death of the USSR in 1991, the global decline of Russia, and the economic rise of the states of eastern Asia have radically altered these geopolitical features. The Eurasian pivot no longer exists.

Now, for an indeterminate period, the pivot is constituted by the United States, the sole global superpower, at the epicenter of the two other economically advanced and/or dynamic regions of the world: the European Union and the economically fast-growing states of eastern Asia.

As for the heirs of the nomads in eastern Asia, Mongolia, or on the periphery of China who were often made sedentary by force, after a period of being overwhelmed, those in the first group are only just beginning, hesitantly and partially, to take their fate in hand again. They are, in any event, far from being at the center of the great changes that have affected the world in the second half of the twentieth century, or those that seem likely to mark the beginning of the new century.

Yet, these peoples on the periphery of the last two empires, and above all Russia, have begun to reconstruct the geography of the region and will surely once again have an impact, notably in terms of population, on the history of central Asia.

Note

1.   See M. Jan and R. Cagnat, *Le Milieu des empires* (Paris: Laffont, 1981).

Appendices

Periodization of Nomad Waves

First phase

Scythians, Sarmatians, Alans, groups of Iranian origin (Indo-Europeans) from the eighth century B.C.-c. second century A.D. In the first centuries A.D., the Turkish-speaking element gradually occupy western central Asia (Turkestan) and eliminate or assimilate the Iranian element.

Second phase

The Hsiung-Nu (Turkic-Mongols) occupy greater Mongolia. Active against China from the fourth century B.C. They form an empire in the third-second centuries B.C.

The Hsiung-Nu drive the Yüeh-chih (Indo-Europeans) westward in the second century B.C. The Yüeh-chih found the Kushan empire (first century B.C.-second century A.D.) from Iran to India.

Third phase

The fourth-fifth centuries see the nomads of High Asia flood over the entire world theater. The To-pa (fourth century) overrun northern China and found the Wei dynasty (368-534) while the Juan-juan (fourth century) constitute a standing threat to the Wei.

Expansion of the Black Huns (fifth century) towards the Near East and Western Europe; and of the Hephthalite (White) Huns towards the Gupta empire (India), which they destroy, and Sassanid Iran, which they ravage.

Fourth phase

After defeating the Juan-juan, the Tu-chueh (Turks) create a vast steppe empire (sixth-seventh centuries), which soon disintegrates. Allied with the Sassanids, they annihilate the Hephthalite Huns, and then ally with Byzantium against the Sassanids. China fights them.

In the sixth century and for the following two centuries, the Avars attack the Byzantine empire and Russia and conquer Hungary where they partly succeed in establishing themselves. They end up being crushed in the ninth century by the Carolingians.

The Bulgars, emerging from central Asia, cross the Danube (fifth century), or certainly some of them do, become slavized and clash heavily with the Byzantine empire. Another section of the Bulgars settle on the Volga.

The Khazar Turks (seventh century) in western Asia and the Uighur Turks in the east form states; the former, one of whose khaghans converts to Judaism, allies with Byzantium; the latter converts to Manichaeism, often allies with China.

Fifth phase

The tenth-eleventh centuries are a time of turbulence in the steppe of High Asia, doubtless for demographic reasons, and nomad waves pour out in all directions.

The Khitans (Khitaï) take northern China (tenth century) and found the Liao dynasty.

The Seljukid Turks make a sensational entry on the Iranian front, which they occupy as far as the border with India (eleventh century). They penetrate into Anatolia. The Pechenegs clash with the Byzantine empire and Kievan Russia (eleventh century). Soon they are followed by the Kipchaks who are unable to overcome the Byzantine empire and harass Kievan Russia.

Pressure from the Turkish-speakers, first with the Ghaznavids (tenth century) in eastern Iran, is soon felt as far as northern India. Establishment of the Mamluk sultanate of Delhi (1206). Finally, coming from Manchuria, the Jurchens conquer northern China (twelfth century) while a section of the Khitans flee and found the empire of the Qara-Khitaï further west (twelfth century).

Sixth phase

In the thirteenth-fourteenth centuries, all the areas hitherto held by the nomads, whoever they were, as well as much of the Eurasian continent come under the domination of the Mongols who form the largest universal empire in history.

Timur extends the heritage of Genghis Khan in his own way, but, after his death (1405), his successors are unable to retain it for long. But Babur conquers India in 1526 and founds the Mughal dynasty.

Seventh phase

The decline of the warrior nomad societies originating in central Asia begins in the mid-sixteenth century and lasts until the mid-eighteenth century. However, China is conquered by the Manchus (1644). The khanate of the Crimea is annexed only in 1783, and the coup de grâce is given to the Oirots by the Manchu emperors only in the mid-eighteenth century (1758).

Nomad Empires of High Asia

Sixth-second centuries B.C.	Scythian empire (Iranians).
Third-second centuries B.C.	Hsiung-nu empire (Turkic-Mongols).
First-second centuries A.D.	Sien-Pei empire (Mongols).
Fourth-sixth centuries	Juan-juan empire (Mongols).
Sixth century 552- c.582	Tu-chueh empire (Turkic).
Sixth-seventh centuries	Division into two khaghanates: khaghanate of the Eastern Turks (582-657), khaghanate of the Western Turks (582-630).
Seventh-eighth centuries	Second khaghanate of the Eastern Turks (682-744).
Seventh-ninth centuries	Tibetan expansion in central Asia; zenith of the Tibetan empire (755-797). Collapse of the Tibetan empire (c. 842).
Eighth-tenth centuries	Uighur (Turkic) khaghanate, Manichaean by religion (740-840), destroyed by the Kirghiz (Turkic).
840-924	Kirghiz empire of Mongolia.
1130/1135-1211	Empire of the Qara-Khitaï (Mongols, Buddhist by religion.
Thirteenth-fourteenth centuries	Genghiskhanid empire.
Fifteenth-sixteenth centuries	Uzbek (Turkic) empire founded by Abu'l Khayr (1428-1468),

	consolidated by Shaybani Khan (1451-1510).
Fifteenth century	First Oirot empire (Mongols) which reaches its zenith with khaghan Esen (1439-1455).
1690-1758	Second Oirot empire (Mongols). Decline, after 1699, under attacks from the Manchu emperors.

Sites of Waves of Invasions

Europe (mainly Russia, central Europe and the Balkans)
>   Huns fifth century
>   Avars sixth-ninth centuries
>   Bulgars seventh-eighth centuries
>   Hungarians ninth-tenth centuries
>   Pechenegs eleventh century
>   Kipchaks (Cumans or Polovtsis) Twelfth century
>   Genghiskhanids thirteenth-fifteenth centuries
>   Osmanlis after the fourteenth century

Middle East (mainly Iran, Afghanistan, Asia Minor, Mesopotamia). *Egypt* (and Syria) remain under Mamluk control (thirteenth-sixteenth centuries; military slaves mostly Turkish-speaking).
>   Ghaznavid Turks eleventh-thirteenth centuries
>   Selkjukid Turks eleventh-twelfth centuries (thirteenth for those from Konya)
>   Khorezm Turks twelfth-thirteenth centuries
>   Genghiskhanid Turks thirteenth-fifteenth centuries
>   Timurid Turks fourteenth-fifteenth centuries
>   Shaybanid Turks from fourteenth century
>   Osmanlis from fourteenth century

China (northern China except for the Mongol and Manchu dynasties)
>   Hsiung-nu fourth-third centuries B.C.-second century A.D. (Turkic-Mongols)
>   To-pa fourth-fifth centuries (proto-Turks)
>   Juan-juan fifth-sixth centuries (Mongols)
>   Khitans (Mongols) tenth-twelfth centuries

Jurchens (originally from Manchuria) twelfth-thirteenth centuries
Yuan dynasty (Genghiskhanid Mongols) thirteenth-fourteenth centuries
Oirots fifteenth century (Mongols)
Manchu dynasty seventeenth century (1644)
Oirots seventeenth century

India

In 480, the Hephthalite Huns destroy the Gupta empire.

India then experiences five centuries of external peace.

But from the eleventh century to the sixteenth century, invasions and/or occupations by nomads or the Islamized direct descendants of nomads succeed one another.

The conquerors are almost all of Turkish-speaking origin, and culturally highly iranized.

Mahmud of Ghazni launches a first series of raids: 1001-1026.

The last Hindu king of Delhi is dethroned in 1197 (the Hindus return to power only in 1947).

The Mamluk sultanate of Delhi is established in 1206 (Mohamed Gur).

Timur takes Delhi (1398).

The Turkic-Afghan Kaji dynasty occupies the Deccan in the fourteenth century.

In 1526, conquest of India by the Chagatai Babur, driven out of Samarqand by the Uzbeks.

Creation of the Mughal dynasty (1526-1858).

Chronology

209	The Hsiung-nu acquire an outstanding leader: Motun.
201	*The Han (206 B.C.-9 A.D.)* begin to fight the Hsiung-nu nomads systematically.
Second century	The Scythians split into two kingdoms. Mithridates IV Eupator, king of Pontus, defeats the Scythians.
Second-first centuries	The Sarmatians advance towards the northern Caucasus.
198	A treaty is signed between the Han and the Hsiung-nu.
175-165	The Yüeh-chih are driven out of Kansu towards Bactriana.
Second century	The Goths, Germans from the steppes (Ostrogoths and Visigoths), between the Volga and the Danube.
167 and 166	The Hsiung-nu enter Chensi and Kansu (China).
159	Hsiung-nu incursion.
144	Hsiung-nu incursion.
142	Hsiung-nu incursion.
140-130	Invasion of Iran by the Yüeh-chih (Tokharians).
129	Hsiung-nu incursion.
127	The Han counter-attack and take the Ordos.
121	Second defeat of the Hsiung-nu, north of the Ordos.
119	Third defeat of the Hsiung-nu who withdraw their capital north of the Gobi.
115-60	The Chinese and the Hsiung-nu fight for control of the steppes leading to the Tarim basin.
102-101	The Chinese secure control of the whole steppe along the oases as far as the Ferghana basin.
60	The Han control all the steppe as far as modern Kirghizstan.
53	Disaster inflicted by the Parthians on the Roman legions under Crassus at Carrhae (Syria).

51	The Hsiung-nu, much weakened, are made into vassals. They split into the Northern Hsiung-nu and the Southern Hsiung-nu.

A.D.

11	The Northern Hsiung-nu attempt to revert to the status quo ante while the Southern Hsiung-nu remain under Han protection.
25-c.223	*Later Han dynasty.*
c.50-c.230	Kushan empire created by the Yüeh-chih from the Aral Sea to the Punja (Kanishka: 78-103).
63	The Scythians defeated by the Roman legions withdraw from the Chersonesus and fall back northward.
74	The Han defeat the Northern Hsiung-nu.
89/91	Hsiung-nu defeated in Mongolia.
107 and 123	Hsiung-nu return offensive.
220	End of the Han dynasty.
224	Sassanid empire in Iran.
220-280	*Time of the Three Kingdoms.*
Third century	In the middle of the third century, the Scythians of the Crimea and along the lower Dniepr disappear, driven out by the Goths.
265-419	*Southern Tsin dynasty* (China).
304-415	The Southern Hsiung-nu invade China.
317	The descendants of the Southern Hsiung-nu overthrow the Western Chin dynasty and found the first non-Chinese dynasty. The Chinese rulers take refuge at Nanking.
c.374	The Black Huns drive the Alans out of the area north of the Black Sea.
376	The Visigoths ravage the Balkans and attack the Goths.
386-535	Northern Wei dynasty of nomad (To-pa) origin.
395	*Constantinople, second capital of the Roman Empire.*

402-410	The Juan-juan on the Chinese border.
424	Juan-juan raid against the Wei (northern China).
429	Another raid by the Juan-juan.
440	Beginning of the invasions by the Hephthalite (White) Huns into Iran and India.
443-447	The Black Huns ravage Thrace and Greece.
445	Attila proclaimed supreme leader of the (Black) Huns.
448	Juan-juan raid against the Wei (northern China).
451	Battle of the Catalaunian Plains (or Châlons) (near Troyes, France), between Attila and the Roman general Aetius. Attila withdraws.
452	The Huns in Italy.
453	Death of Attila. Collapse of the Huns and their empire in Europe.
458	Juan-juan raid against the Wei (northern China).
476	*Fall of Rome.*
480	The Hephthalite or White Huns destroy the Gupta empire (India). The Bulgars between the Danube and the Caspian.
484	The Sassanid emperor (Iran) killed by the Hephthalite Huns.
552	Foundation of the empire of the Tu-chueh (Turks) over all of central Asia.
558-570	The Avars driven out of Asia penetrate into Europe and some settle in Hungary.
c.570	The Tu-chueh and Sassanids defeat the Hephthalite Huns and divide up Transoxiana and Khorasan between them.
c.582	Division of the Tu-chueh empire into two khaghanates: one in the west, one in the east.

c.582-1060	The Khazars create a powerful state northeast of the Black Sea.
582	The Avars attack Constantinople.
601	The Avars driven back by the Byzantines. Conflicts between the Avars and Byzantium last from 582 to 796.
601	The Eastern Tu-Chueh attack China.
618-907	*Advent of the T'ang dynasty.* Offensive policy against the nomads.
619	Avar raid on the Byzantie empire (Constantinople).
622	*Hegira* (beginning of Islam).
624 and 626	The Tu-chueh attack China.
626	The Avars and Sassanids vainly besiege Constantinople.
630	Fall of the khaghanate of the Western Turks.
632-680	*Initial Muslim expansion led by the Arabs: from Libya to the frontiers of India and central Asia.*
657	Fall of the khaghnate of the Eastern Turks.
658	The T'ang control central Asia as far as modern Turkestan.
665	Beginning of Tibetan expansion into central Asia.
678	The Arabs vainly besiege Constantinople.
679-680	The Bulgars cross the Danube and found a state.
680-751	*Second phase of Muslim expansion: from Spain to the frontiers of the T'ang empire.*
681	Second khaghanate of the Eastern Turks.
682-720	Frequent incursions by the Eastern Tu-chueh into China.
717	Second unsuccessful siege of Constantinople by the Arabs.
744	End of the secod khaghanate of the Eastern Turks.

745	Uighur empire in central Asia.
751	Defeat of the T'ang at Talas (Kirghizstan) by the Arabs and their Qarluq (Turkic) auxiliaries.
755-797	*Zenith of the Tibetan empire in central Asia.*
763	General withdrawal of the T'ang from central Asia.
c.780	Foundation of Greater Bulgaria on the Volga.
786-809	*Harun al-Rashid; zenith of the Abbassids.*
794-796	Pippin and Charlemagne defeat the Avars.
803	Disintegration of the Avars in central Europe.
811	The Bulgars defeat the Byzantines at Adrianople.
840	The Uighur empire annihilated by the Kirghiz.
840-924	Kirghiz kingdom in High Asia.
842	*Collapse of the Tibetan empire in central Asia.*
864-865	The Bulgars and the Serbs converted to Christianity under the influence of the Byzantine empire.
874	*Iranian dynasty of the Samanids.*
899	The Magyars cross the Carpathians and enter Hungary.
900-955	The Magyars (Hungarians) ravage Western Europe, especially Italy.
907-960	*China divided into "five dynasties."*
910	The Magyars in Germany.
915	Incursion of the Pechenegs into Russia.
916	Foundation of Khitan kingdom in Mongolia.
921	Foundation of the Ghaznavid dynasty.
922	Unification of the Volga Bulgars.
924	The Magyars in Burgundy.

926-947	The Khitans occupy northern China (Liao dynasty).
926-954	The Magyars in Lorraine, Champagne, and Burgundy.
934-1091	The Pechenegs harass Byzantium.
947	The Khitans take northern China.
955	After ravaging part of Western Europe, the Magyars are defeated by the German emperor Otto I at the battle of Lechfeld. They are soon converted to Christianity.
965-967	Svatoslav, prince of Kiev, defeats the Khazar empire.
969	*Conquest of Egypt by the Fatimids.*
979	*Much of China reunited by the Sung.*
999	The Karakhanids, an Islamized dynasty, make themselves masters of Transoxiana.
Late tenth century	Empire of the Karakhanids.
Early eleventh century 1001-1026	Mahmud of Ghazni launches a series of expeditions against India.
Early eleventh century	Muslim conquest of northern India.
1026	Pecheneg onslaught on the Byzantine empire.
1028-1029	The Seljukid Turks attack Iran.
1036	The Pechenegs defeated by the prince of Kiev.
1040	The Seljukids overcome the Ghaznavids.
1054	Beginning of raids by Kipchaks (also called Cumans or Polovtsis) in Russia.
1059	The Seljukids take Ispahan.
1061	Pecheneg raids on the Byzantine empire.
1064	New Pecheneg raids on the Byzantine empire.
1071	Byzantine defeat at Manzikert (Armenia) inflicted by the Seljukids.
1081	Foundation of the Turkish kingdom of Konya (until 1237).
1087	Pecheneg raid on the Byzantine empire.
1088	New Pecheneg raid on the Byzantine empire.

1089	New Pecheneg raid on the Byzantine empire.
1091	Byzantines and Kipchaks form an alliance and defeat the Pechenegs. The "Rus" defeat the Kipchaks, with the help of the Pechenegs.
1093	The Kipchaks sack Kiev.
1099	*Capture of Jerusalem by the Crusaders.*
1103	Vladimir Monomakh and Sviatopolk II ally against the nomads.
1111, 1113, 1116	Vladimir Monomakh victorious against the Kipchaks.
1120-1126	The Jurchens (called Chin in Chinese) conquer northern China held by the Khitans (Liao dynasty). Some of the latter migrate westward and establish a state called Qara-Khitaï (c.1135).
1122	Destruction of the Pechenegs.
1125	Unification of the Kipchaks in southern Russia.
1150	Destruction of Ghazni by the Ghurids.
1157	Fall of the Seljukids of Iraq.
c.1165	The Muslim Karakhanids overthrown in Transoxiana by the Qara-Khitaï who are Buddhists.
Between 1155 and 1167	Birth of Genghis Khan.
1176	Byzantine defeat by the Seljukids at Myriakephalon.
1183	The "Rus" defeat the Kipchaks and capture their khan.
1185	Campaign by prince Igor Sviatoslavich of Novgorod-Seversk against the Kipchaks (*The Lay of Igor*).
1187	*End of the Ghaznavid empire.*
1194	End of the Seljukids of Iran, defeated by the Qara-Khitaï.
1197	Defeat of the last Hindu king of Delhi.
1206	Beginning of Mongol conquest under Genghis Khan.

	Great *Khuriltai* (Grand Council):Genghis enthroned khan.
	Mamluk sultanate of Delhi.
1207	Submission of the forest peoples: Oirots and Kirghiz.
1209	Uighurs and Tanguts recognize Genghis Khan's suzerainty.
1210-1220	Apogee of empire of Khorezm.
1211	Beginning of the campaign against the Chin (Jurchens) of northern China.
1213	Capture of Lo-yang.
1215	Surrender of Beijing.
1217	The conquest of China is entrusted to Mukali.
1218	Meeting of a great Khuriltai.
	The Qara-Khitaï are defeated by Jebe.
	The Mongols invade Korea.
1220	Successful campaign against the state of Khorezm. Capture of Bukhara and Samarqand.
1221	Conquest of Chensi by the Mongols. Destruction of Balkh and Merv and conquest of Afghanistan.
	Mongol victory over the Georgians.
	Victorious battle of the Indus where Genghis Khan is present.
1222	Capture of Chang-an by the Mongols. The Russians and the Kipchaks overwhelmed at the battle of Kalka by the Mongols.
	Destruction of Herat by the Mongols.
1227	Death of Genghis Khan.
1229	Meeting of a great Khuriltai: election of Ogodei as new Great Khan.
1230-1231	Conquest of Iran by the Mongols. Khorezm forces are annihilated.
1232	Capture of Kaifeng, last capital of the Chin, this time definitively defeated after twenty-two years of resistance to the Mongols.

1235	Meeting of the great Khuriltai: four-pronged military operation: Korea, southern China (Sung), Middle East, Europe.
1237-1242	Extended campaign by Batu in the Caucasus, Russia, and central Europe.
1236	Conquest of Georgia by the Mongols.
1237	Destruction of the kingdom of Greater Bulgaria. Destruction of Riazan (northern Russia). Capture of Ispahan.
1238	Campaign in Transcaucasia. Destruction of Moscow and above all Vladimir.
1240	Conquest of Armenia. Destruction of Kiev.
1241	Conquest of Korea. Victory over the Poles and Germans at Leignitz. Victory over the Hungarians at Sayo. The Mongols' forward forces are not far from Vienna, when news arrives of the death of the Great Khan, and Batu retraces his steps in 1242 to Karakorum.
1243	Victory over the Seljukid army at Erzinjan (eastern Anatolia).
1246	Guyuk elected Great Khan.
1248	Death of Guyuk.
1250	*The Mamluk dynasty, predominantly Turkish-speaking military slaves, from Ukraine (1250-1516), is founded in Egypt.*
1251	Election of Mongke as Great Khan.
1254-1279	Conquest of southern China(Sung) by the Mongols.
1255	Death of Batu, first khan of the Golden Horde.
1256	Hulagu invades Iran.

1258	Sack of Baghdad and mass killings. Conquest of Szechuan by the Mongols.
1259	The Mongols take Cracow.
1260	The Mongols take Aleppo and Damascus. Khubilai elected Great Khan and establishes his residence at Beijing. Battle of Aïn Jalut (Syria); for the first time, a Mongol unit is defeated by the Mamluks of Egypt.
1262	Conflict between the ilkhans of Iran and the Golden Horde.
1266	Mongol incursion into Byzantine Thrace.
1267-1368	*Mongol Yuan dynasty in China.*
1274	Failure of the first Mongol landing in Japan.
1277	The Mongols penetrate Burma.
1280	The Mongols masters of the whole of China.
1281	Failure due to a typhoon of the second Mongol landing in Japan.
1285	The Mongols checked in Vietnam.
1287	Burma is conquered by the Mongols and becomes a vassal (1297).
1290	End of the Delhi Mamluks.
1293	Mongol expedition against Java.
1294	Death of the Great Khan Khubilai.
1295	Ghazan becomes ilkhan of Persia (where the Mongols convert to Islam).
1296-1297	Mongol attacks in northern India.
1299	Osman I (reigns until 1326).
1302	End of the Seljukid sultanate of Anatolia.
1312	Under Ozbeg, the Golden Horde converts to Islam.
1327	Mongol expedition into northern India.
1336	End of the Mongols of Iran.
1346	The Ottomans cross the Dardanelles.
1361	The Ottomans take Adrianople.

1368	The Chinese drive the Mongols out. The Yuan dynasty replaced by the Ming dynasty (1368-1644).
1370	Tamerlane (Timur Leng) comes to power.
1379	Tamerlane conquers Khorezm.
1380-1385	Tamerlane conquers Iran.
1380	Short-lived Russian victory over the Mongols at Kulikovo.
1382	The Golden Horde returns to the attack. Tuqtamish destroys Moscow and Vladimir.
1387	First victory of Tamerlane over Tuqtamish and the Golden Horde.
1389	Battle of Kosovo. The Ottomans dominate the Balkans.
1389-1413	Reign of Bayazid I.
1391	Tamerlane ravages the lands of the Golden Horde and the White Horde. Another victory by Tuqtamish.
1395	Tamerlane leads another expedition against the Golden Horde. Final defeat of Tuqtamish on the Terek.
1396	Christian armies defeated at Nicopolis by the Ottomans.
1398	Tamerlane takes Delhi.
1399	The grand duke of Lithuania fights the Golden Horde unsuccessfully in Ukraine.
1402	Tamerlane defeats the Ottoman sultan Bayazid at Ankara.
1405	Death of Tamerlane on his way to China.
1406	Restoration of the Ak Koyunlu and the Kara Koyunlu (Turkish-speakers).
1412-1468	Abu'l-Khayr, founder of Uzbek power.
1414	The Ottomans defeat a Christian army sent by the West at Varna.
1430	Foundation of the khanate of the Crimea.
1445	Foundation of the khanate of Kazan.

1448	The Ottomans defeat the Hungarian Jan Hunyadi at Kosovo.
1450	Esen, ruler of the Oirots (Mongols), crosses the Great Wall and defeats the Ming.
1453	*Fall of Constantinople, taken by the Ottomans.*
1456	Foundation of the khanate of Astrakhan.
1470	Unification of the Mongols (descended from Tului) with Dayan Khan and Altan Khan (until 1583).
1480	Ivan III declares the end of the "Mongol yoke," but it proves premature.
1492	*Granada taken by the Christians.*
1502	End of the Golden Horde. *Foundation of the Sefavid dynasty.*
1520-1566	*Suleyman the Magnificent.*
1521	Khan Salib Giray of Kazan defeats the Russian army.
1526	Babur conquers India and founds the Mughal dynasty (1526-1858).
1542	Khan Dayan defeats the Ming.
1552	Ivan IV, known as the Terrible, takes Kazan.
1556	Destruction of the khanate of Astrakhan. *Akbar emperor of India.*
1571	Deviet Giray, khan of the Crimea, burns Moscow.
1582	*The Russians begin the conquest of Siberia.*
	After the sixteenth century, the history of central Asia becomes merely regional history. Only the khanate of the Crimea, in the west, abutting on the Ottoman empire, remains an important power.
1600	Destruction of the khanate of Sibir.
1615-1650	Kirghiz resistance to Russian penetration.

1644	Conquest of China by the Manchus (who reign until 1911).
1690	Galdan Khan, ruler of the Oirots, lays siege to Beijing, but is unable to take it.
1696	Capture of Azov by Peter the Great at the expense of the khanate of the Crimea.
1699	The Manchus counter-attack and defeat the Oirots.
1710-1876	Last Shaybanids at Kokand (Ferghana).
1713	Russian protectorate over the Kazakhs.
1736-1747	Nadir Shah establishes a short lived empire in central Asia.
1742-1775	*Revolt by Pugachev (supported by the Tartars and the Kazakhs).*
1757	Final defeat of the Oirots inflicted by the Manchus. *Annexation of Sinkiang by China.*
1782	The Russians annex Yakutia.
1783	The khanate of the Crimea is annexed by Russia.
1744-1844	After a series of hard-fought campaigns, destruction and abolition of the Kazakh khanates.
1858	Official end of the Mughal empire (essentially powerless since 1717).
1866	Bukhara a Russian vassal-state.
1873	Khiva annexed by the Russians.
1876	Kokand annexed by the Russians.

Annotated Bibliography

On central Asia or High Asia: The leading book is undoubtedly D. Sinor (ed.), *History of Early Inner Asia* (Cambridge: Cambridge University Press, 1987). See also M. G. Levin and L. P. Potapov, *The Peoples of Siberia* (Chicago: University of Chicago Press, 1964); this has chapters dealing with the Scythians, Sarmatians, and other Indo-Iranians, not including the Mongols, by a series of experts, and covers the period from the first millennium B.C. to the end of the twelfth century A.D. See also Denis Sinor, *Introduction à l'étude de l'Eurasie centrale* (Wiesbaden, 1963) and his other writings, including "The Inner Asian warriors," *Journal of American Oriental Society* (1981): 133-144. René Grousset, *L'Empire des steppes* (Paris: Payot, 1939) (Eng. tr. D. Sinor and M. MacKellar, *Conqueror of the World*, London, 1967), was a pioneering work covering the whole area from the very beginning down to the end of the age of the conquering nomads. L. Kwanten, *Imperial Nomads: A History of Central Asia 500-1500* (Leicester, 1979). B. Spuler (ed.), "Geschichte Mittel Asiens," in *Handbuch der Orientalistik*, vol. V, 5 (Leiden, 1966). See also *The History of the Civilizations of Central Asia* (Paris: Unesco, 1992), vol. 1.

On the Scythians: Herodotus, Book IV; T. T. Rice, *The Scythians* (London).

On the Huns: O. Maenchen-Helfen, *The World of the Huns* (Berkeley and London: University of California Press, 1973); E. A. Thompson, *A History of Attila and the Huns* (Oxford: Clarendon Press, 1948) and F. Altheim, *Attila et les Huns* (Paris, 1952); L. Hambis, *Attila et les Huns* (Paris, 1972); Ammianus Marcellinus, *The Later Roman Empire (344-378) Books I to IV* (Harmondsworth: Penguin, 1986).

On the Turkic-speakers of central Asia: W. Barthold, *Zwölf Vorlesungen über die Geschichte des Türken Mittelasiens* (1932-1935, reprint Heidelberg, 1962) (Eng. tr. from Russian by V. and T. Minorsky: Bartold, W. *Four Studies on the History of Central Asia*

(Leiden: E. J. Brill, 1956-1962); by the same author: *Histoire des Turcs d'Asie centrale* (Paris: Maisonneuve, 1945), and *Turkestan down to the Mongol Invasion*, trans. H.A.R. Gibb (London: Luzac & Co., 1928, E. J. W. Gibb Memorial Series, New Series, No 5). S. Julien, *Documents historiques sur les T'ou Kiue*, translated from the Chinese (Paris, 1877). E. Chavannes, *Documents sur les Tou-Kiue occidentaux* (Saint Petersburg, 1903). Palaeo-Turkic inscriptions in Thomsen, *Inscriptions de l'Orkhon déchiffrées. Mémoire de la société finno-ougrienne* (Helsinki, 1896). D. M. Dunlop, *History of the Jewish Khazars* (Princeton: Princeton University Press, 1954). J. R. Hamilton, *Les Ouighours à l'époque des Cinq Dynasties d'après les documents chinois* (Paris, 1955). C. MacKerras, *The Uighur Empire according to the T'ang Dynastic Histories* (Canberra: Australian National University, 1972).

On the nomads preceding the Mongols: P. Diaconu, *Les Petchénègues au Bas-Danube* (Bucharest: Editions de la l'Académie de la République Socialiste de Roumanie, 1970); *Les Coumans au Bas-Danube aux XIe et XIIe siècles* (Bucharest: Editions de la l'Académie de la République Socialiste de Roumanie, 1978). P. Browning, *Byzantium and Bulgaria. A Comparative Study across the Early Medieval Frontier* (London, 1971).

On the Turks who, like other warrior nomads, visibly fascinate the author so much that he sometimes loses his critical faculties, see J. P. Roux, *Histoire des Turcs* (Paris: Fayard, 1984).

On the Mongols, there is a vast literature. In addition, the sources for it are in a very large number of languages: Chinese, Persian, Arabic, Armenian, Georgian, Greek, Latin, Russian, etc. For the context, see *The Cambridge History of China* (1982); *The Cambridge History of Islam* (1970); *The Cambridge History of Iran* (1968) and, of course, *L'Encyclopédie de l'Islam* (Leiden). These works are also the fundamental ones on the Turkic-speakers and their impact on the Muslim world.

Among the strictly Mongol documents or other texts, one is reduced to: *The Secret History of the Mongols*, trans. F. W. Cleaves (Cambridge, Mass.: Harvard University Press, 1982), *Histoire secrète des Mongols*, French tr. M. D. Even and R. Pop (Paris: Gallimard, 1994), and *The Mongol Chronicle*, Altan Tobeï, C. R. Bawden (Wiesbaden, 1956). Among the Chinese sources: *Histoire des campagnes de Gengis Khan*, trans. P. Pelliot and L. Hambis (Leiden, 1951). The *Yuan-Shi* (History of the Yuan dynasty) has been only partly translated into German by F. E. Krause: *Gingis Han* (Heidelberg, 1922).

Among the Persian sources: Ata Malik al-Juwayni, *Ta'rikh-i-Jahan-gusha*, 1260 (Eng tr. J. A. Boyle, *History of the World Conqueror*, 2 vols. [Manchester: Manchester University Press, 1958]) and above all F. Rushiedden, *Djami At-Tawarikh* (Compendium of Histories), trans. M. d'Ohsson: *Histoire des Mongols depuis Tchinguiz Khan jusqu'à Timour Bey*, 4 vols. (The Hague-Amsterdam, 1834) (Eng. tr. J. A. Boyle, *The Successors of Genghis Khan* (London, 1971).

Arabic sources: Ibn al-Athir, *Chronicles*.

Russian sources: *The Laurentian Chronicle* records events in Kiev and Galicia; *The Nikon Chronicle* records events in Riazan, Tver, Suzdal, Vladimir, etc.

Armenian sources: D. E. Dulaurier, *Les Mongols d'après les historiens arméniens*, J.A.S. Série 5, XI, Paris 1858 and 1860 (pp. 273-322); Gregory of Akanč, *History of the Nation of Archers*, trans. R. P. Blake and R. N. Frye (Cambridge, Mass.: Harvard University Press, 1954).

The Franciscans left eyewitness accounts of the greatest importance such as those of John of Plano Carpino and William of Rubruck, which are collected with others by Christopher Dawson in *Missions to Asia* (London and New York: Sheed & Ward, 1955). Two outstanding twelfth-century travelers should also be read: Ibn Battuta, *The Travels of Ibn Battuta A. D. 1325-1354*, Eng. tr. with revisions and notes from the Arabic text edited by C. Defrémery and B. R. Sanguinetti by H. A. R. Gibb, tr. completed with annotations by C. F. Beckingham (Cambridge: Cambridge University Press, 1958-1994, for the Hakluyt Society), and Marco Polo, H. Yule, and H. Cordeier (eds.) *The Book of Ser Marco Polo the Venetian concerning the Kingdoms and Marvels of the East* (London, 1903, reprint 1963). See also Michel Jan, *Voyageurs en Asie centrale* (Paris: Bouquins/Laffont, 1992).

The views of Europeans are reflected in the chronicles about the Mongols collected by Gian Andri Bezzola, *Die Mongolen in Abendländischer Sicht (1220-1270)* (Berne and Munich: Francke Verlag, 1974). See also D. O. Morgan (ed.), *Medieval Historical Writing in the Christian and Islamic Worlds* (London, 1982). And Bertold Spuler, *History of the Mongols Based on Eastern and West-*

ern Accounts of the Thirteenth and Fourteenth Century, Eng. tr. H. and S. Drummond (London: Routledge and Kegan Paul, 1972).

Among older works: D'Ohsson, *Histoire des Mongols* (4 vols.) (The Hague-Amsterdam, 1834-1835). More recently: B. Spuler, *The Mongols in History*, Eng. tr. G. Wheeler (London: Pall Mall Press, 1971) and J. J. Saunders, *The History of the Mongol Conquests* (London; Routledge and Kegan Paul, 1971). B. J. Vladimirtsov, *Le Régime social des Mongols*, Fr. tr. M. Carsow (Paris: A. Maisonneuve, 1948) is still stimulating. G. Vernadsky, *The Mongols and Russia* (London, 1953). If one were to read only one book on Genghis Khan and the imperial rise of the Mongols at the beginning of the thirteenth century, then that book should be: Paul Ratchnevsky, *Cinggis-Khan. Sein Leben und Wirken*, 1983, translated into English as *Genghis Khan, His Life and Legacy* (Oxford: Blackwell, 1992).

Finally, for general works, essential reading is: Owen Lattimore "Inner Asian Frontiers of China," *American Geographical Society*, 1940, reprinted by Oxford University Press, 1988, and "Studies in Frontier History" in *Collected Papers, 1928-1938* (Oxford: Oxford University Press, 1962). See also Léon Wieger, "Textes historiques," *Histoire politique de la Chine jusqu'en 1912*, 2 vols, Hien Hien, 1929.

On Timur:

Sources: Nizam al-Din *Zafer name*, 1404, *Livres des victoires* (in French) (tr. Petis de la Croix, Paris, 1722). Ibn 'Arabshah, *Etrangeté du destin sur les ventures de Timour* (Paris, 1658) (Fr. tr. P. Vattier). Ali (Sharaf al-Din), Yazdi, The History of Timur-Bec translated into French by Petis de la Croix and rendered into English by John Darby (London: J. Darby, 1723). W. Fischel, *Ibn Khaldun and Timour* (Berkeley, 1952). Timour, *Mémoires (Malzufat)* (Paris: Langles, 1787). *Instituts (Tuzuhat)* (Paris: Langles, 1787).

The wars of Tamerlane and Shah Rokh in western Asia according to the Armenian chronicles of Thomas of Medzoph, Brussels, 1860. R. G. de Clavijo, *Narrative of the Embassy of Ruy Gonzalez de Clavijo to the Court of Timour, at Samarcand, AD 1403-6* (London, 1859). L. Kehren, *Tamerlan. L'empire du seigneur de fer* (Neuchâtel, 1978). Jean Aubin, "Comment Tamerlan prenait les villes," *Studia islamica* (Paris, 1963): 83-122. M. M. Alexandresca-Dersca, *La Campagne de Timour en Anatolie* (Bucharest, 1942; London, 1977).

Babur, *The Babur-nama in English: (Memoirs of Babur)* Eng. tr. from the original Turkic text by A. S. Beveridge (London: Luzac & Co., 1921) 2 vols.

On a more recent period: Maurice Courant, "L'Asie centrale aux XVIIe et XVIIIe siècles. Empire kalmouk ou Empire mandchou," *Annales de l'Université de Lyon*, N. S. 26, 1912. C. R. Bawden, *The Modern History of Mongolia* (London: Weidenfeld and Nicholson, 1968). J. F. Baddeley, *Russia, Mongolia, China*, (London: Macmillan, 1919) 2 vols.

Seymour Becker, *Russia's Protectorates in Central Asia: Bukhara and Khiva 1865-1924* (Cambridge, Mass.: Harvard University Press, 1968), and Hélène Carrère d'Encausse, *Réforme et révolution chez les musulmans de l'Empire russe*, Cahiers de la Fondation nationale des sciences politiques, preface by Maxime Rodinson (Paris: Armand Colin, 1966). A. Bennigsen and C. Lemercier-Quelquejay, *L'Islam en Union soviétique* (Paris: Payot, 1968) (Eng. tr. *Islam in the Soviet Union*, London: Pall Mall Press, 1967) and, by the same authors: *Les musulmans oubliés* (Paris: Maspero, 1981). Martha Olcott, *The Kazakhs* (Stanford: Hoover Institution Press, 1987). The author, a Russian-speaker, is a fine expert on contemporary central Asia.

Index